NORFOLK
AT WORK

The saw mill at the Briton Brush Company, Wymondham, 1924.

BRITAIN IN OLD PHOTOGRAPHS

NORFOLK AT WORK

NEIL R. STOREY

This book was first published in 1997 by Sutton Publishing Limited
Phoenix Mill · Thrupp · Stroud · Gloucestershire · GL5 2BU

This edition published in 2000 by
Lucas Books

British Library Cataloguing in Publication Data
A Catalogue record for this book is available from the British Library

ISBN 0-95347-206-X

Half-title photograph: a beautiful pair of Norfolk plough horses, pictured in the late 1940s wearing harness made by James Frederick Southey, a saddler and harness-maker of Great Yarmouth, in 1892; Title page photograph: a Thetford farm carrier with his horse and cart, *c*. 1908.

Typeset in 10/12pt Perpetua.
Typesetting and origination by
Sutton Publishing Limited.
Printed in Great Britain by
J.H. Haynes & Co., Sparkford.

This book is dedicated to the members past and present of the Royal Norfolk Agricultural Association.

Officials of the Royal Norfolk Agricultural Association, 1928. Left to right: Sir H. Upcher, Sir H. Overman, Mr A. Lewis, HRH the Duke of Gloucester, Mr J.F. Wright, H.P. Gowan, the Lord Mayor of Norwich, the Rt Revd Bertram Pollack, Bishop of Norwich.

CONTENTS

Harvestmen at Swanton Morley, 1894.

The roundsman and his cart for Richard Francis Proudfoot, the Bacton butcher, *c.* 1908.

INTRODUCTION

In the introduction to the *General History and Description of Norfolk* by William White, his directory of the county produced in 1845, he says of Norfolk: 'It is celebrated for the diversity and high cultivation of the soil; for the abundance and excellence of its agricultural productions; for its crape, bombasin, and other manufactures of silk and worstead; [and] for its herring and mackerel fisheries.' His words were well founded as the trades he mentioned existed in the county for hundreds of years. Indeed the county's early importance and wealth were derived from wool and the weaving trade, and the fine medieval churches scattered across Norfolk (more than in any other county in Great Britain) bear testimony to this. The cloth trade flourished here for over 500 years and is traditionally associated with Worstead, the village from which the fabric takes its name. Sadly, the trade was decimated by the introduction of machine mills, particularly in the north of England, during the Industrial Revolution. The last true Worstead weaver, John Cubbitt, died in 1882. Despite a valuable trade in Norwich shawls, horsehair-weaving in Wymondham and the production of hemp in the Lophams, the weaving trade had disappeared in Norfolk by the First World War.

The photographs in this book illustrate many contrasts. Sadly many show aspects of Norfolk's historic and traditional trades, established over hundreds of years and once an integral part of the county's life, but now all but faded into the past. Gone are the 'Herring Heydays' of Scots fisher-girls and drifters; gone are the once-mighty shoe factories of Norwich which employed so many thousands of people; gone are the many long-established breweries like Morgans, Steward & Patteson, and Bullards, whose chimneys once provided distinctive landmarks on the city skyline; and gone are the days when Kelly's directory listed hundreds of blacksmiths, farriers, wheelwrights and millers. In contrast, it is refreshing to see that some of the old businesses are still flourishing, and it is interesting to trace their history and note the diversifications they have had to employ to survive so long. Many of these businesses are local 'institutions' and some are household names, whose roots can be found in the eighteenth and nineteenth centuries.

A fascinating insight into social and working history may be derived from a study of the little shops and their staff in the days when butchers and fishmongers displayed their wares in the open air, and tradesmen visited door to door with horse-drawn carts or on bicycles to deliver everything from daily consumables like milk and bread to paraffin and saucepans.

Many of the changes illustrated in this book are comparatively recent but no less important for that, such as the astonishing changes in transport over the last two hundred years. King Charles II, commenting on the road surfaces during a visit to the Earl of Oxnead in 1671, said that 'Norfolk ought to be cut into strips, to make roads for the rest of the kingdom'. How appropriate then, that the first turnpike road was established here in 1694, heralding a web of such roads across the county. Norfolk's transport systems have always been heavily influenced by the numerous navigable waterways, both rivers and canals, plied by wherries carrying the county's goods out to the harbour towns and beyond. In more recent years the Broads have provided both employment and income derived from the holiday and boating industries. The presence of the canals, providing such ease of movement around the county, meant that railways were treated with less enthusiasm than in some other counties. Norfolk was one of the last English counties to establish a railway system, starting in 1844 with the Yarmouth and Norwich Railway. In a contemporary trade directory further schemes under parliamentary consideration at the time were mentioned in rather derogatory terms: '. . . some will, no doubt, be sanctioned, and others postponed or abandoned; indeed we think several of them could never be made profitable speculations.'

A Norfolk gamekeeper and his dog, c. 1905.

One of the mighty Norfolk black-sailed wherries, once so common on our Broads, glides along the River Ant, *c.* 1885.

It is interesting to observe the various modes of transport on water, roads and railways as they developed over the years, and to see how the entire character of the county and its landscape changed with them. In the mid-nineteenth century the driving force was the horse, with steam-powered vehicles and trams being introduced in the big towns around the turn of the century, and eventually making way for the internal combustion engine in all its forms.

Some developments, such as those in the public utilities, are very surprising. For example, homes and shops in the county were being fitted out with gas lighting and appliances as early as the 1820s. Electricity was established in Norwich in the 1890s with sub-stations rapidly springing up across Norfolk by the early 1930s. Some 700 square miles of the county (approximately 30 per cent) was supplied with electricity – the largest area supplied by a municipal undertaking in Great Britain.

During the depressed inter-war years a massive development and improvement programme was undertaken by the city and rural district councils in an attempt to provide work for the hundreds of jobless ex-servicemen. Victorian slums were cleared, a new city hall and public baths built and huge parks created, with gardens, bowling greens and boating ponds. The country's first council housing estates were built in Norwich, the first house being let in October 1920. About five thousand houses were constructed on six large estates on the outskirts of the city, each house being rented at a net rent in 1930 of 5*s*, plus 3*s* 3*d* rates, an additional 6*d* for running hot water and 2½*d* for 'electric current'.

Public water supplies in the form of reservoirs were to be found in Norwich and in the larger towns from the late eighteenth century but most people in rural areas depended on wells until the turn of the century. Water towers, pumping stations and treatment plants for piped water supplies followed shortly after, but mains sewers and inside toilets remained luxuries for many people, especially those in more rural areas, until after the Second World War.

Agriculture has always played an important role in Norfolk's history, especially during the 'Golden Age of Agriculture' when vast numbers of sheep were driven to the shearing festivals, and local landowners such as 'Turnip' Townsend and Thomas Coke of Holkham were at the forefront of agricultural progress. Townsend was renowned for his innovative four-course crop rotation on his Raynham Hall Estate, while Coke instigated the famous sheep shearing festivals. In those days there were over 50,000 agricultural labourers in Norfolk and farming was a way of life, not just an occupation. All the members of the family became involved from an early age and people came from miles around to help at certain times of year, especially at harvest time. Life was dominated by the seasons. Farming was hard, physical work, with many tasks being done by hand. In those days horses provided additional power, especially for heavy work such as ploughing, when teams of two or three Suffolk Punches were used — but woe betide the ploughman who didn't understand his horses.

The way we work affects all our lives and developments in this area have perhaps been the greatest contributing factor to the appearance of Norfolk today. Changes occur so rapidly that the past's way of life appears increasingly remote, and many aspects are disappearing for ever. I hope this book offers everyone the opportunity to look back and learn from the way people lived and worked in Norfolk over the last 150 years. I leave you with a once popular harvest song of the Norfolk scythemen, which is still relevant today, especially when you meet some of the characters at county shows throughout the year.

> We Norfolk lads are bold and rough,
> We love the sound of early horn,
> And our rosy cheeks and sinews tough,
> We owe to Sir John Barleycorn.
>
> Keep yew orl a'troshin'!

Neil R. Storey
Norwich, 1997

Colonel V.N. Lockett, President of the Royal Norfolk Agricultural Association, with winners of the shepherds' and long service awards at the Royal Norfolk Show, Norwich, 1946.

THE FARMING YEAR

A proud ploughman with his shire horse stallion at Dersingham, 1912. Doubtless they tilled a good few miles together. It would take a man one day to plough 1 acre with a horse-drawn plough, and in doing so he would walk about 4 miles. For hundreds of years the horse was the principal driving force on the land, and before the Second World War there were about one million working horses in Norfolk alone.

A Norfolk ploughman sets his plough to the field for the first time in the new farming year, *c.* 1908. Traditionally in Norfolk 'Plough Monday' falls on the first Monday after Twelfth Night: 'it bids out with the plough: the worst husband is last'. Much custom surrounded this important day: plough-boys were 'initiated' by kneeling in the fields and having the soles of their boots tapped with the oldest ploughman's wish-spoon or stone. 'Fool Ploughs' were dragged round villages by boys with blackened faces to 'much hollering'.

George Bailey of Church Farm, Rickinghall, leads his twenty-year-old horse Prince through the village after drilling sugar-beet with a hundred-year-old seed drill in the early 1960s. Farmers in Norfolk were reluctant to replace their working horses with tractors. George said: 'I was brought up with old things and old ways and I like them. When I am driving a tractor I find myself shouting "Whoa".'

A ploughing match at Plumstead, March 1939. Left to right: F. Barnes, F. Grout, G. Gee, H. Thaxter, H. Hazelwood, J. Lubbock, R. Gee. Such matches to sharpen and prove the ploughman's skill were regularly held across the county until shortly after the Second World War when gradually the horses were superseded by tractors. Similar matches may still be seen at good country shows today.

Old meets new as plough horses and caterpillar-tracked tractors seed a field on a west Norfolk farm shortly after the Second World War. In those days, when there was still petrol rationing and modern machinery was treated with suspicion and contempt in certain quarters of the Norfolk farming fraternity, there were still an estimated 538,000 horses working the land in the county.

Jimmy Davison, 'king of the mole catchers', netting sparrows at Swanton Abbot, *c.* 1925. He was one of about twenty-five vermin destroyers operating in the county during the 1920s, using a wide variety of nets, traps and herbal concoctions to rid fields, farms and gardens of all manner of pests. Little was wasted: rabbits and sparrows were made into pies, while mole and rabbit fur was made into clothing, especially 'tippets', which were a type of hand-muff.

'Clapper boy' Billy Dan Boldero at work with his bird scarer in a field near Castle Acre shortly after the First World War. No hours were set for his employment – he simply worked from sun up to sun down for a penny a day. The ash wood clappers were made in three pieces, the two tongues being half the length of the handle and all the parts loosely jointed with pieces of leather.

Walter Amies, the Witton shepherd, watches over his flock during the spring lambing season, 1912. Beside him is his constant companion: the sheepdog used to round up and drive the flock. The crook was used to catch the sheep – the shepherd simply hooked it around the sheep's leg and pulled it towards him until he could get hold of it.

John Aves & Son, contract sheep dippers of Wrenningham and Wymondham, at work on a south Norfolk farm, *c*. 1900. By law farmers had to dip their sheep in a disinfectant solution to control scab and infestations in the fleece. Often the village policemen would be present or at least formally informed to ensure the law was complied with.

Spectators, farmers and stock breeders gather round the pens at the Hempton Green Sheep Fair, 1949. This town was once rightly famous for its three large annual fairs held on Whit Tuesday, 22 November and the first Wednesday of September. The first two were cattle fairs, the latter a large sheep fair. Its origins are traceable back to the days of Hempton Priory, founded in the reign of Henry I for Augustinian canons to whom King John granted the right to hold an annual fair.

Ernie Griffin, Jimmy Strike and Oswald Griffin, armed with stools and special pails, set off to milk the cows on River Farm, Honing, c. 1934. The milk trade had stabilised well in the county, especially after the Milk Marketing Board was set up in 1933 to purchase all the milk produced on farms.

Red Poll steer Elmham Morris, owned by Sydney Morris of Manor Farm, Gately, North Elmham. This was the heaviest beast aged under two years at the Norwich Fat Stock Show held at the Agricultural Hall, November 1932. It weighed in at 13 cwt, 1 qtr, 16 lb.

What a porker! Large black sow Depwade Duchess III, champion at the Oxford County Show, 1936. She was bred and owned by Mr Frederick Alexander of Laurels Farm, Pulham Market, Diss.

The Royal Norfolk Agricultural Show at King's Lynn, June 1910. First held in 1847, the Royal Norfolk Show has long been the highlight of the Norfolk farming year, a chance to show prize stock, wonder at agricultural innovations and mardle about how the season has fared. For many years the show was itinerant, being held at various sites around the county, but from 1953 it has been held at Costessey, on a permanent site purchased for it by the Royal Norfolk Agricultural Association. As well as the Agricultural Show every June, various other events take place on the showground throughout the year.

A display showing comparative barley yields using 'Kainit' fertiliser at the Wayland Show, c. 1910. Barley has been an important crop since it was first brought to Britain during the neolithic period. It grows well on East Anglia's chalky soil and has been the principal cereal crop in Norfolk since the time of the Roman occupation; it is used in the production of beer, bread and meal. All across the county in summer fields still sway with this rich versatile crop.

Sir George Chamberlain DL, Lord Mayor of Norwich during the First World War, photographed with the committee and officials of the Royal Norfolk Agricultural Show held at King's Lynn in 1919. At this time he was President of the Royal Norfolk Agricultural Association.

Judging pony carts at Acle Show, 1912. Agricultural fairs and shows have been held in Norfolk since the sheep shearing festivals instigated by Coke of Holkham in the late eighteenth and early nineteenth centuries. Pride and competitiveness led to keen participation and many farming communities established their own shows. In some cases a group of parishes clubbed together, the annual show being held in each parish in rotation.

Agricultural Wages (Regulation) Act, 1924.

AGRICULTURAL WAGES

Minimum and Overtime Rates of Wages for Workers in Agriculture at present in force in

NORFOLK

I.—ORDINARY MALE WORKERS.

Years of Age.	Rates per Week.	Hours per Week.	OVERTIME RATES (per Hour).	
			Weekdays.	Sundays.
	s. d.	Christmas	d.	d.
21 and over	30 0	week 40.	9	11
20 and under 21	28 0	Any other	8½	10½
19 „ „ 20	26 6	week in	8½	10½
18 „ „ 19	25 0	Winter 48.	7½	9½
17 „ „ 18	20 0		6	7½
16 „ „ 17	16 0	Any week	5	6
15 „ „ 16	13 0	in Summer	4	5
Under 15	10 0	50.	3	4

II.—SPECIAL CLASSES.

TEAMSMEN, COWMEN, SHEPHERDS AND YARDMEN in addition to the above wages shall receive, in respect of duties in connection with the immediate care of animals, the following amounts :—

TEAMSMEN, SHEPHERDS AND YARDMEN of all ages
COWMEN of 18 years of age and over, and } 5s. 6d. per week
COWMEN under 18 years of age (if in sole charge of animals)
COWMEN „ „ „ (if not in sole charge of animals) 3s. 0d. „

SHEEP-TENDERS AND BULLOCK-TENDERS in addition to the above wages shall receive, in respect of duties in connection with the immediate care of animals, the following amounts :—

18 years of age and over - 4s. 6d. per week
Under 18 years of age (if in sole charge of animals) - 4s. 6d. „
„ 18 „ „ (if not in sole charge of animals) - 3s. 0d. „

Overtime rates as above. No duties in connection with the immediate care of animals rank as Overtime Employment.

III.—FEMALE WORKERS.

Years of Age.	MINIMUM RATES. (per Hour).	OVERTIME RATES (per Hour).	
		Weekdays.	Sundays.
	d.	d.	d.
18 and over	5	6½	7½
17 and under 18	4	5	6
14 „ „ 17	3½	4½	5

EMPLOYMENT TO WHICH OVERTIME RATES APPLY.

(a) All employment in excess of 6½ hours on one weekday in each week as agreed between employer and worker.

(b) All employment on a Sunday and on Christmas Day.

(c) All employment in excess of 40 hours in the week in which Christmas Day falls, 48 hours in any other week in winter and 50 hours in any week in summer (excluding all hours which are treated as hours of overtime employment and, in the case of workers of the special classes, excluding also employment in connection with the immediate care of animals).

NOTES.

1. The above rates will operate as from 3rd March, 1929, and will continue in force up to and including 28th December, 1929.

2. For the purpose of the above rates " summer " shall be the period from the first Monday in March to the first Sunday in November and " winter " shall be the rest of the year.

3. Deductions from the above rates may be made only in cases where a cottage, milk, potatoes, or board and lodging are supplied. A cottage may be reckoned for the purpose at 3/ per week less any rates paid by the occupier, Milk at current wholesale price, Potatoes at wholesale price at the time the main crop was lifted, and board and lodging at 15/- per week in the case of workers aged 18 years and over. (Lesser sums for younger workers.)

Forms of application for a permit exempting a worker from payment at the minimum rates (in cases of workers who by reason of any physical injury or mental deficiency or any infirmity due to age or to any other cause, are incapable of earning the minimum wage) may be obtained from the Secretary of the Norfolk Agricultural Wages Committee, **Old Parcels Office, Burrell Road, Ipswich, Suffolk.** Complaints as to non-payment of the prescribed rates should be addressed to the Secretary, Ministry of Agriculture and Fisheries, 7, Whitehall Place, London, S.W. 1.

N.B.—The above particulars are merely a summary of the Orders, and for full details of the legally binding provisions, reference should be made to the actual Orders, copies of which may be obtained from the Secretary of the Committee at the above address.

March, 1929.

1/29. (2581). Wt.— 2005. 3,875. 3/29 Wy. & S., Ltd. Gp. 2.

Hand-bill showing agricultural wages in Norfolk, March 1929.

Members of the Norfolk Agricultural Workers' Union on the march at Castle Acre during their strike in 1923. Recession had hit Norfolk hard between 1920 and 1922 and farmworkers' wages had been reduced from 42s to 25s for 52 hours' work a week. In March 1923 over ten thousand men came out on strike. Despite the farmers' sympathy for their workers' plight, most could not afford to pay more and were forced to bring in 'blackleg' labour. At the end of the strike more than two hundred labourers faced criminal proceedings for trespass and intimidation but Ramsay Macdonald intervened and the men went back to work at 25s with no victimisation.

George Edwards, founder of the Eastern Counties Agricultural Labourers' and Smallholders' Union in 1906 and legendary Labour campaigner for the rights of agricultural workers, stands victorious with his agent Edwin Gooch (left) after winning a 2,118 majority in the South Norfolk by-election of August 1920. He served as a loyal MP for many years.

Harvestmen enjoying a welcome respite from their back-breaking labours, sharpening their scythes at Houghton St Giles, *c.* 1890. A good harvestman could mow an acre of corn a day and a team of harvestmen working in line could cover a considerable area. All harvestmen worked under the leadership of the 'Harvest Hainer' or 'Lord of the Mow', who was often the oldest and most experienced harvestman. He was appointed by the scythemen to negotiate the rate of pay with the farmer and all the men would follow him, not stopping to sharpen their blade, drink, or take a break until he did so.

Corn harvesting on Burrell Hammond's Farm on the Brampton Hall Estate, *c.* 1910. A single scytheman would cut a swathe around the field to allow access for the horse-drawn binder.

Carting the hay at Mulbarton, *c.* 1910. Ladies in their sun-hats raked the hay as the men pitched and loaded the stocks on to the cart. The cries of the 'holla-gee boy' moved the horses along in time with the pitchers to keep the momentum going.

George Balding, the farmer of Beech Farm, Thorpe Market, helping to build the hay into a stack, *c.* 1950. Before the days of mechanical balers the hand-built haystack or rick-yard was common to every Norfolk farm. Built with considerable skill to a height of about 25 ft, each stack was capped off with a beautifully thatched 'roof'.

The end of a good day's 'troshing' (threshing) at Keswick Hall, the seat of John Henry Gurney Esq., 1912. Towards the end of the season threshing machine contractors would be hired, their traction engines and drums becoming a familiar sight rattling and hissing along the Norfolk lanes. The stacks were then thrashed from the rick-yard, usually at the rate of a stack a day, being separated into grain for sale, chaff for cattle feed and straw which passed up the elevator for stacking.

Pictured on a Norfolk farm at the turn of the century, these workers of all ages, from scythemen and lady-rakers to trace-horse boys and small children, whose job it was to chase and catch vermin at harvest time, are ready for the Horkey. This traditional harvest home celebration in Norfolk is best summed up in the old local rhyme:

Heed ye not the uncouth lingo,
Quick the polished spit display,
Broach the cask of nut-brown stingo,
Harvest home's a holiday.

Soft fruits have always been a successful and popular crop in the county, and here we see raspberry pickers on Arthur E. Parfitt's market-garden farm at Foxley in about 1908. The cart moved alongside the pickers, collecting the filled baskets and issuing empty ones. Once the cart was fully loaded, it would trot the 2 miles to North Elmham station from where the fruit was taken on to the London markets.

Tobacco harvest at Feltwell, *c.* 1913. Over the years a great diversity of crops has been grown on Norfolk's rich soil, but this was probably the most unusual. Tobacco was grown in this area as part of the Methwold Reclamation Scheme until the First World War, but massive competition from the United States meant it was no longer a viable investment.

Enjoying the autumn sunshine, these smiling girls are harvesting sprouts at Manor House Farm, Bintree, during October 1936. The farm was owned at this time by Algernon William Garrod.

Broccoli, another winter crop, being packed and loaded at A.W. Garrod's farm at Bintree ready for the London markets, October 1936.

Hoeing beet at Rippon Hall Farm, Hevingham, *c*. 1910. The farm belonged to William and Thomas Case. Left to right: -?-, William Vincent, Charles Willimat, John Waller, Ben Griffin, -?-, George Farrow. William Vincent was the verger at Hevingham Church for almost forty years.

Dutch workmen hoeing sugar beet at Cantley, *c*. 1912. Influenced by Dutch growers, who imported some of their own labour, and encouraged by the development of sugar refining in the county, Norfolk farmers were persuaded to grow sugar beet, an investment which has proved good ever since.

A 'chop and blower' forage harvester driven by a John Deere tractor on a mid-Norfolk farm, *c.* 1949. Horse-power slowly declined in Norfolk from just after the Second World War, the gentle giants being replaced by tractors which became increasingly reliable, more widely available and affordable as time progressed. With their introduction a whole community way of life on the land disappeared.

Never before considered as a viable possibility, the ultimate innovation on the farm at the time was the introduction of night harvesting. Here tractors with headlamps and illuminated machinery lift sugar beet at Southrepps in 1948.

CRAFTS & TRADES

Len Roper at his workshop on Bank Loke, North Walsham, carves the town's Second World War memorial plaque. It lists the names of the local men who fell in that conflict and was hung in the parish church in 1950. Len's considerable skills in wood carving and crafting were learned from his apprenticeship at Cornish & Gaymer, the local ecclesiastical carvers.

Shearing sheep at Cavick, Wymondham, *c.* 1895. The process and the tools remained more or less unchanged for hundreds of years and no doubt shearing skills were widely practised across Norfolk over the 500 years that the wealthy wool trade was the mainstay of the county's industry.

Billy Poll, the foreman of the Friarscroft weaving factory at Wymondham, pictured with his shears beside the fleece of a freshly shorn sheep, *c.* 1895. As a general rule, one man using manual shears could shear eighteen short-wool or forty long-wool half-bred sheep in a working day.

Albert Tyler, the last of the North Lopham weavers, at work on his loom, *c.* 1910. Before the Industrial Revolution such looms were to be found in every town and village across Norfolk. Weavers' cottages, with their distinctive wide windows to maximise daylight hours, may still be found today. The wealth and importance of this incredibly profitable industry, which was centred on Norfolk in the middle ages, are testified to by the fact that more medieval churches were built here than anywhere else in Northern Europe. These splendid buildings were all built from the profits from wool and weaving – truly Norfolk's 'Golden Fleece'.

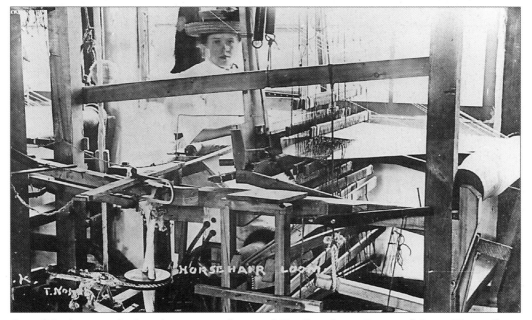

One of the looms at the horsehair weaving factory of Hovell & Co. on Friarscroft Lane, Wymondham, *c.* 1900. At one time there were more than 600 looms weaving bombasins and crapes in Wymondham alone. The decline of the trade was slow but steady and by 1910 it was almost non-existent in the town.

Charles Rolingson at work in his forge at Shelfanger, 1954. A village blacksmith for over forty years, he was one of the last of his kind. Blacksmiths were once to be found in every town and village across the country. Before the war he regularly shod more than a hundred horses a week but by the 1950s he was lucky to shoe that many in a year.

Henry Taylor at his workshop and forge, *c.* 1904. With him are his daughter and two sons who followed him into the business as carpenter, builder, wheelwright and general smith at Great Poringland. Unusually Mr Taylor was proficient in both wood- and metal-working disciplines: it was more common for blacksmithing and wheelwrighting to be separate trades. Their businesses were usually to be found close together as their skills needed to be combined to produce items such as wooden wheels with metal hubs and rims, and other farm equipment such as ploughs.

Fitting a tyre was a skilled task, as shown here at Matlaske in 1929. Clifford March, who made the tyre in the forge, watches as Jesse Riseborough and John March 'set' the hot tyre to the wheel with large hammers. Mr March (senior) uses a watering can to cool down the tyre and prevent severe burning of the felloes (parts of the rim of wheels).

Thomas Button of Tharston, one of the last true Norfolk wheelwrights, pictured in his workshop, 1947. He is surrounded by the tools and works of his trade from hubs and spokes to felloes. Note the adze, a type of axe where the plane of the blade is at right angles to that of the axe. It was not a commonly used tool but in his skilled hands it was essential in the initial rough shaping of a hub.

George Knights, saddler and harness maker, stands in the doorway of his shop with his son and his apprentice to his left at Ludham in 1911. His window is full of bits and tack, while the halters and collars by the door, crafted by his own hands, demonstrate his skills. The business was passed to him by his father Samuel before the turn of the century. By the 1920s the gradual decline in horse-power had encouraged him to diversify to include shoemaking, ironmongery, grinding, and making tar and paints. By the time Albert took over the business in the 1930s this diversification had paid off and the business was flourishing, now including sporting goods and fishing tackle.

John 'Jack' Hewitt making a new binder canvas in his workshop on Church Plain, North Walsham, *c.* 1964. The horse collars indicate his true profession – he was apprenticed to a saddler and harness maker in the town in 1918. In 1927 he opened his own shop and later leased some branch shops at Bacton, Tunstead and Happisburgh. Even as mechanisation took over he remained one of the last true traditional saddlers in the county, taking in extra work making agricultural equipment and leather goods. He finally retired in 1964. A true craftsman, he is still alive today in his nineties. 'Keep yew a'troshin', Jack!

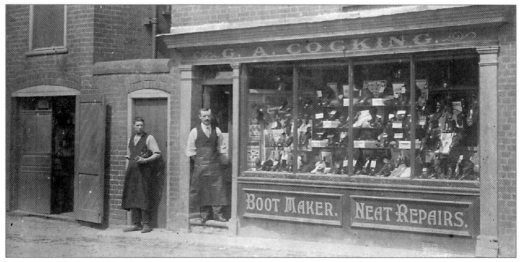

George Albert Cocking, bootmaker of The Green, Martham, *c.* 1909. This is a rare skill today but in the 1920s there were hundreds of boot and shoemakers across the county, with their vast array of tools including cutting knives, scorers and punches. The decline of horse-power between the wars saw an increase in their numbers as saddlers and harness makers were forced to branch out into associated trades to keep their businesses going.

Farman Brothers', Thatch Yard, Salhouse, *c.* 1912. This photograph was taken in the early years of the brothers' ownership of the business and shows the neatly stacked rows of sways, liggers and broaches – all the fixings for thatched roofs. Joseph Farman had started his small basket-weaving business at the turn of the century and passed it on to his sons as a going concern which they developed in the 1930s as thatchers and reed merchants. They also made wattle and garden fences.

The ancient art of the Norfolk thatcher pictured during the 1930s. The first sway is in position, secured by hooks to the rafters and then bound in with reed. The march of progress meant that the thatcher's art was another consigned to the nostalgic past. In 1890 there were seventy-seven thatchers in Norfolk, trading near every town and village; by 1937 this number had declined to just over fourteen. Today a mere handful of very skilled men keep the trade alive.

Robert George Osborne at work on one of his famous wicker hurdles at his workshop in Honing, c. 1912. He passed his business on to his sons, who continued to trade in the 1930s and beyond making baskets, chairs, tables and wicker fences.

Rush weavers and basket makers with some examples of their work at Norfolk Rush & Reed Industries Ltd (incorporating the St Faith's Rush Industry) at Broad Farm, Buckenham Woods, Rockland St Mary, c. 1935.

The ancient art of the cooper was still practised in the breweries and cider factories across the county until the early 1960s. These coopers are at work in their shop at Steward & Patteson's brewery in Pockthorpe, Norwich, in 1963 being watched attentively by a group of visiting Norfolk farmers.

The Wramplingham wood turner and brushmaker at work, surrounded by the tools of his craft, in 1958. The craftsmen in some rural villages, whose skills had in many cases been handed down from generation to generation for many years, preserved the community's self-sufficiency up to relatively recent times. Although most of these village industries are long gone, craftsmen working in small workshops may still be encountered in the more remote parts of Norfolk.

David Mackenzie Amiss, printer of Market Street, North Walsham, *c.* 1900. He is wearing the traditional white apron of the printer; to his right is his brother-in-law Trivett Reed and to his left is the shop-boy Sidney Cannell. Printing was a traditional trade and apprentices had to serve for a number of years, learning the skills of compositing, blocking and letterpress – all done by hand in those days.

The precision working of an experienced scale-maker at Josiah Fisher & Sons Ltd of Banham. This long-established firm dates back to the end of the last century when Josiah Fisher, the farmer of Moor Farm in Banham, also acted as a qualified adjuster of weights and measures for the locality.

Hillingdon Church organ being removed for restoration by W.A. Boggis of Roydon near King's Lynn in May 1953. The organ was built in about 1756 by John Snetzler.

ON THE ROADS

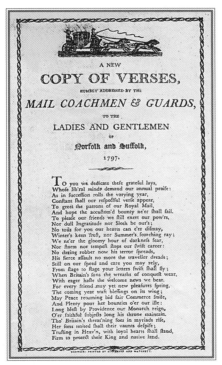

From the days when highway robbery was quite literally that, comes 'The Coachman's Lament' of 1797.
Coaching was far from the romantic idealised image we have of it today: most journeys over a reasonable
distance were uncomfortable and often arduous, especially for those people who travelled on the outside of the
coach. In the summer they were covered in the dust thrown up from the dusty turnpike roads by the horses
and in the winter they suffered whatever the weather could throw at them. On one perishingly cold night,
the coachman of the Norwich mail-coach was found 'frozen solid and quite dead at the reins'; apparently
the coach only arrived at its destination because the horses knew the route so well.

The 'Lobster' Coach ready to set out for Cromer from the Maid's Head Hotel, Norwich, *c.* 1909. Harking back to the days of turnpikes and coaching, this service was revived by Sir Thomas Cook just after the turn of the century. Calling en route to Cromer at St Faiths, Roughton and Aylsham, the service was described as 'a Gentleman's whimsey'; it was never really practical and ceased just before the First World War.

One of the Wymondham stone pits, *c.* 1900. Norfolk boasts the first turnpike in the country, laid between Wymondham and Attleborough in 1694, and the stone pits in this area supplied the materials for the new network of turnpike roads that sprang up everywhere. Wymondham flints and binding silt were used for turnpikes in Norfolk and the whole country until the widespread adoption of macadamised road surfaces in the late 1930s.

One of the last horse-drawn tu'penny buses at Thorpe Green in 1895. It belonged to the Norwich Omnibus Co. Ltd. Once a popular means of transport in the city and the suburbs, the buses became outmoded with the coming of trams to Norwich in 1900.

A road gang and steamrollers laying in the flints for the new road surface near Wymondham, *c.* 1908. The roads in those areas of Norfolk not served by turnpikes were notorious for their appalling conditions. The upkeep of the roads fell to the parishes through which they crossed until the inception in 1889 of Norfolk County Council, which took responsibility for the main roads under the 1888 Local Government Act. By the time this photo was taken the county had over 1,400 miles of main roads and was spending £13,000 a year on surfacing work.

Laying tram lines in front of the Maid's Head Hotel, *c.* 1899. The tram system spread rapidly throughout the city and comprised 19 miles, 2 furlongs and 100 yards of rails with a power station on Duke Street. It was completed in 1900 at a total cost of about £330,000.

The last operating horse-drawn tram on Gorleston High Street, July 1905. The Gorleston horse-drawn service began in March 1875 and continued until it was replaced by electric trams on 4 July 1905. Owing to the technical difficulties for tramlines crossing Haven Bridge in Great Yarmouth, the county's towns did not have an integrated transport system until motor buses were introduced in the 1920s.

Tram terminus, Orford Place, Norwich, c. 1910. Opened on 30 July 1900 the Norwich Tramways were considered a major achievement and a great improvement to Edwardian Norwich. The initial routes around the city itself were rapidly extended out to Unthank Road, City Road, Aylsham Road and the Towse station. The trams in the city proved popular until the 1930s when motor buses began to replace them. The last tram service in Norwich ran on 10 December 1935 from Orford Place to the tram sheds in Silver Road.

Henry Southgate's milk cart, *c.* 1912. He proudly boasted 'Pure Milk from Own Cows', which he kept at Cliff Farm off the Lowestoft Road. His dairy depot was at 146 Bells Road in Gorleston whence his roundsman left with the cart to deliver milk around the town. Many goods were taken around by cart every day, each delivery man or hawker being recognisable by his call.

Edward Hutton's general dealer's cart with his roundsman Bob Buck, pictured in Bacton Road, North Walsham, *c.* 1912. The general dealer's cart offered all manner of pots, pans and earthenware for the kitchen as well as many household utensils and goods ranging from spoons and brushes to buckets and picture frames.

At the turn of the century every self-respecting business had its own delivery carts, roundsmen, stables and staff. The Norwich Co-operative Society Ltd was no exception with four carts delivering coal, coke, briquettes and oil as well as seeds and roots. Photographed at the stables on All Saints Green is the fifth cart which did the bread round. The freshly baked bread would be loaded on to the cart around the corner at the old Queen's Road bakery in Ashby Street for delivery round the streets of the city.

Frederick Arthur Blyth, the oil merchant of 34 Oak Street, Norwich, promised swift delivery of oil or paraffin to any part of the city. With the two-gallon can in the cart and the single-gallon can hanging from the front wheel, his progress on a rainy day could be tracked by the rainbow-sheened puddles in the streets caused by the drips from his cans.

This is the Honing and district postman, *c.* 1912. Some rural parishes had several villages several miles apart within their bounds, all served by one or two postmen who would make their deliveries twice every weekday and once on Sundays. It must have been hard work, especially if they had to deliver parcels by heavy wooden cart. The coming of bicycles and pneumatic tyres must have seemed like a godsend to them.

Marham post office, *c.* 1910. At this time Robert Parlett was sub-postmaster and, typically in such rural areas, his premises also acted as the village grocers. This wonderfully composed scene shows the mail-cart from the post and sorting office at Downham Market on its rounds to the sub-post offices in the surrounding villages, whence the village postmen would pick up the letters for their rounds.

Three Guist postmen, Messrs P.E. Clark, S. Thompson and T.C. Kimber, pictured with their delivery bikes and sidecars, were the first to receive National Safety First Diplomas, presented by Sir Thomas Cook MP in March 1938. Also pictured are Mr A.N. Diamond, the headmaster at Dereham School, and Mr T.C. Vincent, the postmaster at Guist.

Another feature of the roads of yesteryear was the shop-boys doing 'short' delivery rounds from a variety of shops. This lad is standing proudly by his new bicycle bearing the well-known name Sewell & Page, the North Walsham butchers, in about 1912. The boys would be sent out to deliver orders and purchases rather than to hawk the products round the streets. Each lad was recognised by his whistle as he came up the road.

The steam lorry of Edward J. Edwards, public works and sewerage contractors, 1928. This lorry used to be a common sight around Norwich and district, delivering tar, flint and gravel from the depot on Plumstead Road. The company produced some 250 tons of gravel daily.

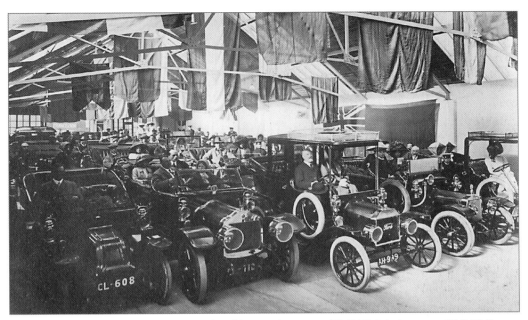

A festival of cars that would now be considered 'vintage' at Henry 'H.G.' St John's garage, 96/102 Regent Road, Great Yarmouth, c. 1911. This photograph backs up his claim that he had a 'Garage for 70 Cars'. No doubt he supplied many of the vehicles seen here which he sold 'at manufacturers' prices'. By 1937 the garage had expanded and was open day and night as motor engineers, offering overhauls, repairs and a garage for 400 cars!

As the number of drivers of all manner of vehicles increased, it became apparent that some formal instruction in the use of such motors, basic mechanics, road law and safety was desperately needed. Just after the First World War Mann Egerton, motor engineers of Norwich, established the first driving school in the country. In those days dual control quite literally meant that – note the two steering wheels.

This heavily laden lorry is the delivery truck for Moss & Potter, importers and bonders of wines and spirits, of White Hart Street in Thetford and Brandon, *c.* 1913.

Speaker van, *c.* 1937. This van was once familiar to residents in the Coltishall, Wroxham, Frettenham and Buxton Lammas areas. It used to drive around the county lanes announcing local events from fêtes to royal proclamations, and was also a fine advertisement for the Central Garage, and the radio and electrical engineers run by Mr C.G. Cooke.

Men of the Norwich City Works Highways Department at work with early pneumatic drills and a compressor in Denmark Road, *c*. 1932. Before the First World War Norfolk County Council Highways Department employed about 700 men, but as the war progressed the number declined to fewer than 300 and most of its horses and carts were commandeered for the war effort. In 1920 the government gave the county council £100,000 to help with post-war reconstruction. By the time this picture was taken Norwich was a Labour party stronghold and led most of the country in its implementation of labour on its streets, housing and development of parks.

Road gang workers of the Ayton Asphalt Co. Ltd of Browick Road, Wymondham, *c*. 1933. The company was founded by Charles Robert Ayton and had stone pits supplying road surfacing materials all over eastern England. As flint surfacing declined in favour of macadamised surfaces Ayton's company followed suit, becoming road surfacing contractors and suppliers of asphalt, bitumen dressing and tar, in which they still trade today.

Wait for one bus and fifteen will all come at once! This cavalcade of Eastern Counties coaches lined up along Earlham Road took over a hundred parishioners of the Roman Catholic Cathedral to the reopening and rededication of the Shrine of Our Lady at Little Walsingham in 1931.

Bus with coachwork by 'modern motor body builders' Bush & Twiddy of Sussex Street, Norwich, c. 1925. The roots of this business can be traced back to Edward Bush, a coal dealer who expanded his small business to include light haulage and basic carriage repairs. Later he was joined by his son and the business developed into a coal factors and haulage contractors, and merged with Twiddys to become motor engineers and body builders. Their vehicles will doubtless be remembered by many Norwich residents.

This twenty-seater de luxe saloon coach on a Studebaker 76 chassis was built by Herbert E. Taylor & Co. Ltd, passenger vehicle and omnibus builders, at their Eaton Coachworks at Cringleford, *c.* 1930. Taylors were fine coach builders whose roots could be traced back to Edward Thrower Taylor, blacksmith and wheelwright of Cringleford. The business developed to become 'automobile agents' and engineers, wholesale ironmongers, general merchants and undertakers, all of which services were still on offer in 1937, according to their entry in Kelly's directory.

Norwich Omnibus Co. Ltd drivers and 'clippies' taking a break at their Surrey Street depot in Norwich in the 1930s. The posters show some tempting day trip offers at reasonable prices: 4s to Lowestoft, 2s 9d to Great Yarmouth, 3s 2d to Happisburgh and 3s 6d to Cromer.

Accidents will happen. In the days when vehicles still had a certain amount of novelty value, any mishaps drew large crowds of onlookers. Here in 1937 a No. 80 double-decker has ploughed into the ancient walls of the Norwich Guildhall in the pouring rain. The police were quickly on the scene from their city centre station to keep order.

Harmer & Scott's Bedford pick-up truck in front of their garage at North Walsham, *c.* 1937. As motor power developed, so did the number of garages, many of which were converted from the increasingly redundant blacksmiths' forges although others were purpose-built like Harmer & Scott of Norwich Road, North Walsham. Established in 1921–2 by Frank Mann & Co. Ltd, this business was sold to John Starling in the late 1920s; he combined it with his existing business as cycle agent and motor shop. In turn he sold the whole lot as a going concern to Stuart Harmer and Bill Scott who built the business up into one of the finest garages in the area. They even had the first female petrol pump attendants in the county in the early 1950s. The name Harmer & Scott survived until 1984 when the garage was sold to the Holburn Group as a tyre and exhaust centre.

FENS, WATERWAYS
& BROADS

*Fen workers returning home from the marshes, October 1886. Over their shoulders they are carrying meaks
(short scythes on long poles) for cutting marsh hay. They worked long hard days with water slopping around
the tops of their marsh boots most of the time.*

Setting up a bow net, 'an ingenious contrivance for capturing fish', *c.* 1886. The hoops were stiffened with sticks and then the nets were weighted with stones and sunk in the fish swims which were well known to the experienced old Broadsmen. Many was the tale told by these men who, when setting their nets at dusk or dawn, saw 'hobby-lanterns' or 'will o' the wisps' over the reeds.

An eel fisherman with his net in front of his temporary home, a converted ship's boat with a cabin and stove built on top, *c.* 1885. Such boats were once commonly found nestling in odd corners of the Broads or beside dykes. Eel fishing took place between July and August, during the breeding season. A good-sized eel weighed 6 or 7 lb, and a good catch of eels could weigh up to about 15 stone.

A wildfowler working up to fowl on flooded marshland, *c.* 1885. Most professional gunners lived at Great Yarmouth, during the season rowing off at the crack of dawn from the old quays and boathouses of the North End and Cobholm Island to Breydon Water, which afforded excellent hunting for waterfowl. Their catch was supplied to Norwich poulterers.

A marsh lady leads the carry while poling the marsh hay, *c.* 1885. The dry hay was forked into heaps which were picked up and carried on two poles to the vessels waiting in the dyke. This was the only way to carry marsh hay since carts and barrows would simply sink into the soft marshy ground.

Reeds being unloaded from a reed lighter and stacked, *c.* 1886. Cutting reeds was winter employment for Norfolk marshmen, often working knee-deep in freezing water. The reed was tied in 'fathoms' (bundles) 6 ft in diameter and taken in lighters to convenient high banks where they were stacked and dried. Once dry they would be taken by lighters to staithes and sold at local auctions by the long hundred of 120 fathoms.

This old Broadsman, having gathered in his marsh hay and quanted his flat-bottomed boat from the Broads into Fleet Dyke, South Walsham, pauses for the camera in the early 1920s. His load of sedge or rushes would have been used for thatching or bedding for cows.

Men at work on the flood defences at Brancaster, *c.* 1905. The coastal communities of Norfolk have faced a constant battle against the sea, and acres of land and indeed whole towns and villages have been lost over the years as the cliffs fall and marshes flood. Efforts to combat this threat have resulted in the building of defences and the cutting of ditches along most of the marshes and coastline.

This idyllic scene is Shotesham St Mary water mill in 1910. It was kept at the time by Arthur Aldridge, in whose family it had been for a number of generations. Watermills used to be familiar across the county, many of them standing on sites used for milling since the Domesday Survey of 1087. More than seventy mills survived the Industrial Revolution and continued in operation into this century. Most have since been either demolished or converted into private homes.

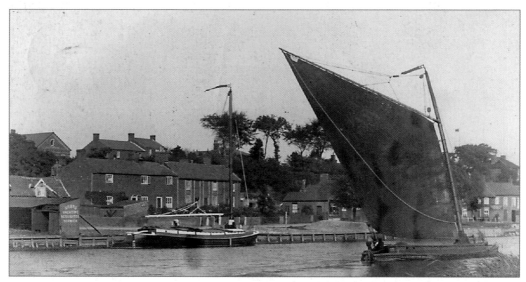

Riverside and moorings, Reedham, 1911. A mighty black-sailed wherry courses the water past Hall's Boat Yard. Hall's had a reputation for building fast wherries and no doubt they have fitted out that new wherry moored alongside. The last Norfolk wherry to be built was the *Ella* in 1912. By 1949 there were to be no trading wherries left under sail.

James Fison & Sons' factory on the banks of the Little Ouse at Thetford, *c.* 1912. James Fison saw his company grow from small beginnings on Bridge Street into a limited concern with numerous outlets and factories at Thetford, East Dereham, King's Lynn, Whittington, Stoke Ferry and Harling Road, trading variously as maltsters, coal, cotton, linseed cake & wool merchants, as well as manufacturers of sulphuric acid and chemical manures. The location of their factory was well chosen, with good river links for trading wherries and railway tracks for the goods wagons which were towed by horses to the Junction station.

Interior of the bagging department at James Fison & Sons' factory at Thetford, *c.* 1912.

The pleasure boats *Clytie* and *Lyndhurst* moored in front of Horning Ferry Inn, one of the finest hostelries on the Broads, *c.* 1905. Steam passenger launches and day boats popularised the Broads from the end of the last century, operating out of boat yards such as Sufflings', Cooke's, Loynes' and Blake's. In addition numerous waterside publicans offered their own boats for pleasure trips.

All aboard! This is probably the most famous of all the Broads steamers, the SS *Jenny Lind*, which plied a leisurely route from Norwich to Great Yarmouth, pictured in about 1910. The boat would be followed along the route by a runner nicknamed 'Billy Bluelight', a famous local character whose real name was William Cullum. More often than not he would beat the boat to Yarmouth, where the passengers would make a collection for him.

The old ferryman on Surlingham Horse Ferry, so named because it could take a horse and cart as well as pedestrians. Like the other horse ferries at Horning and Reedham, it seemed to have been there forever, and each had victuallers and public houses of similar antiquity established beside it.

The Dolphin boats were pleasure craft which worked close to the Heigham Ferry running across the River Wensum to Hellesdon. They were owned by the Norwich Corporation. In 1909 the ferry was made redundant and the boats faded away soon after the Heigham Bridge was constructed by Somerville's Structural Engineers.

The view from Wroxham Bridge along the Bure towards the railway line and station on the right, *c.* 1920. These were the hazy days of the inter-war years, when converted wherries and yachts were used as pleasure craft based around Hoveton and Wroxham. Publicans made sure water-borne clientele could find suitable moorings to encourage trade, such as those on the left for the Horseshoes and King's Head.

Boat yards and moorings at Wroxham, *c.* 1920. The 'Cradle' of the Broads' sailing industry, this area hosted hundreds of yachts and pleasure craft, especially in the regatta season. Beyond them is the boat yard of Ernest Collins & Sons who along with John Loynes, Alfred Collins and George Smith dominated the boat building and hire business in Hoveton and Wroxham up to the 1920s.

The waters were not always calm on the waterways. The great flood of 26 August 1912 caused widespread damage over many miles where rivers and Broads burst their banks. The normally peaceful River Tiffey rose, splitting Cavick Bridge in two at Wymondham. Shortly after the deluge local workmen are pictured setting to work to rebuild the breached bridge.

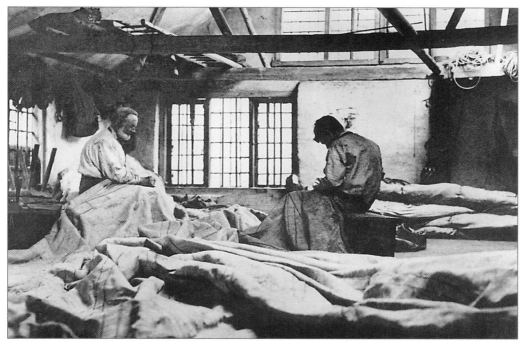

The interior of a Great Yarmouth sailmaker's loft, *c.* 1885. In those days sail was still the principal motive force for seagoing ships, boats and wherries. The sailmaker's craft was still practised in the county at the turn of the century, mostly in Great Yarmouth, by about twenty firms, but by the 1930s this number had been reduced to just a handful of firms making sails for Broads yachts.

Mr F. Dennes, Mr G. Dennes and Mr Giden the foreman pause from their work on a yacht engine at Messrs Banhams' boat yard, Horning, March 1949.

Carrying on the tradition, these workmen at Graham Bunn's boat yard at Wroxham are building some of the last wooden-hulled boats to be constructed en masse for the Broads in 1955. Cruising the Broads is still a popular pursuit but almost all today's holiday-makers use motorised fibreglass-hulled boats. Let's hope that the recent award of National Park status allows the Broads to be preserved for generations to come.

THE RAILWAY

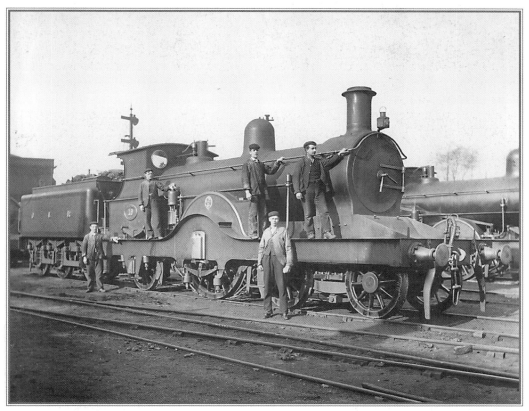

One of the mighty Great Eastern Railway's engines pictured in the 1890s complete with crewmen. These were a familiar sight steaming along the many lines in Norfolk. In the heyday of the railways in Norfolk no village was more than 6 miles from a station and everything from 'passengers to poultry, cattle to corn' found the railways were the quickest and cheapest means of transport especially over long distances.

A masterful block and tackle winching system in action, *c.* 1895. These workmen are constructing one of the many goods sheds at the M&GN goods yard in Norfolk, developed as the trading and goods transport potential of the railways increased at the end of the nineteenth century.

Railway workers, tradesmen and passengers await the arrival of the train at the GER's Harling Road station in 1929. This station was on the Norwich to Brandon line which opened in 1845 and was one of the first railway lines in the county; it provided the first rail link with London. The horse was used for pulling and turning railway coaches.

Young station workers sit down to give their hobnail-booted feet a brief rest at the Midland & Great Northern station at Stalham, *c.* 1910. The large sign advertises two of the popular seaside destinations reached on this line. This was always a well-turned-out station and the thousands of holidaymakers who passed through it were always impressed with the roses over the trellis. It was awarded the best kept station award in 1931.

Washing carriages at the GER's Cromer 'High' station, 1910. Especially in the summer months, train carriages were regularly washed down to remove the dirt and soot accumulated on long journeys. The station itself was described as 'the most beautifully situated station in England', and it was known as the 'High' station because of its situation and the long distance from the beach.

Parcel-car men at Mundesley station, *c.* 1905. Their wagon bears the unusual title of the N&SC Railway. The Norfolk & Suffolk Joint Committee railway was an enterprise operated by both M&GN and GER who were keen to open a new coastal link. Trains first reached Mundesley from the south in 1898 and in 1906 the coastal link to Cromer was completed. Consequently express trains were able to run almost non-stop from London to the Norfolk coast, establishing the massive holiday trade in 'Poppyland' and 'Broadland'.

A newspaper or magazine is always useful to pass the time on long rail journeys and bookstalls and newsagents' stands rapidly appeared at railway stations. This magnificent display is on the W.H. Smith's stall at the GER Vauxhall station, Great Yarmouth, in 1935.

One of the M&GN's permanent way gangs, *c.* 1912. In addition to small localised teams of men maintaining their own lengths of track, the M&GN had two 'mobile' permanent way gangs based at Melton Constable and Sutton Bridge. Here the men pause for the camera with their foreman, Mr Strangleman, on the far right.

The interior of one of M&GN's engineering workshops at Melton Constable in 1936. This was the very heart of the M&GN and occupied a 10 acre site to the south of the village; it had its own narrow gauge railway to convey heavy equipment between departments.

The last day of passenger services on the M&GN railway line through North Walsham, 28 February 1959. An all-too-common feature of the late 1950s and early 1960s was the end of localised railway services through lack of financial support as motor cars and road travel became ever more accessible and practical. Many also fell under Beeching's Axe in 1964–8.

British Railways locomotive 4–4–0 at Thorpe station, with driver, fireman and station staff, 1956. Thirty-odd years after Beeching and the massive railway nationalisation programme, things have turned full circle, with the de-regulation of British Rail into franchise- and business-owned regional railways organised along similar lines to the first railway companies in the early nineteenth century.

A LIVING FROM THE SEA

The crew of the famous herring drifter Fruitful Bough *which made the largest recorded catch ever in one night in British waters — 323½ cran of herring — pictured at Great Yarmouth in 1953. In many ways, however, this picture records the dying years of the herring industry. By 1962 only 21,173 cran were landed and only ten Scottish fisher-girls worked in Yarmouth. In 1968 only five Scottish drifters arrived and by 1969 the tradition had ended — no Scottish boats arrived.*

Cromer fishermen Mr L. Harrison and his two sons mend and ready their crab and lobster pots on the sea front, 1938. They are observed from the railings by the legendary coxwain of Cromer lifeboat, Henry Blogg GC, the most highly decorated man in the history of the lifeboat service.

Sheringham fishermen assist in man-handling the whelk boat *Rose* through the streets from the Crown Inn on the East Cliff, where she had been fitted with an engine, to the slipway where she was launched on Saturday 3 July 1937.

Frank Grice, a well-remembered Sheringham fisherman from an old Sheringham fishing family, pictured on the seafront, c. 1938. He wears a Gansey – a type of Norfolk fisherman's jersey, each one made by hand with specific designs for each coastal town and some designs unique to certain fishing families. These were not simply decorative: a fisherman could be identified by this pattern if he were lost at sea and washed up miles away from home.

Some cold work in December 1938. Mr Robert Cooper, one of the oldest fishermen in Wells and one of the first Sheringham whelkers to settle there, sorts and prepares a consignment of mussels for market.

The fishing fleet, King's Lynn, *c.* 1912. The fleet sailed out from this port to the fisheries of the North Sea which yielded plentiful supplies of sole, cod and smelt. At one time the catches were even larger: the town had a whaling fleet that sailed every spring to Greenland. The whalers' return in August was greeted by the ringing of church bells, and for weeks afterwards the town would reek of boiling blubber.

Crew members of the *Daisy Rock* sort nets ready to put to sea again, *c.* 1920. In those days over a thousand boats followed the herring shoals down the coastline to Great Yarmouth, Gorleston and Lowestoft every year. Thousands of Norfolk and Suffolk men walked to the ports to sign on the crews for the herring voyages. The regular fishermen were described as '. . . tough as whipcord, frugal as hedgesparrows'.

One of the many drifters 'crossing the bar' from the calm harbour waters of Gorleston into the stirring waters of the cold North Sea, *c*. 1912. Drifters got their name from their nets which drifted with the tide. They would put to sea in the afternoon and return the following morning. The nets they shot varied in number between 81 and 101, but always an odd number, and could stretch as far away as 2 miles.

The return of the fishing boats into Gorleston Harbour, *c*. 1920. All chugged away merrily, and when they had all docked the combined smoke from their funnels hung like a smog over Great Yarmouth and Gorleston.

Unloading the herring on to Great Yarmouth quayside, *c.* 1920. In its heyday the herring fleet averaged about 800,000 cran a season (about 900 million fish). A cran was 1,132 herring, weighing about 28 stone, so the catch was in the region of 2,800,000 hundredweight.

Auctioning swills of herring at Gorleston, *c.* 1908. As the boats pulled into the quay a swill of herring would be thrown on to the quayside and picked up by boys who carried it down to the bowler-hatted auctioneers as a sample – so that the catch would be ready for auction as soon as the boat docked.

The purchased herring, fresh off the boat, is sorted and packed on the quayside, *c.* 1921. Behind them horse-drawn carts and lorries wait to carry the catch off to the gutting and curing yards.

Scots fisher-girls gutting herring in the fairlanes at Great Yarmouth, *c.* 1920. Wearing their distinctive tarpaulin aprons, men's boots and brightly coloured shawls, the girls worked in teams of three, gutting, sizing and throwing the fish into the baskets behind them at an incredible rate. One girl (they were all called girls regardless of age) was timed as gutting 57 fish in 1 minute.

The teams of girls would assist one another when their baskets were full, taking the fish to the barrels, as pictured here at Gorleston, *c.* 1905. When at the barrel two would return to gutting while the other remained to pack. For years their pay remained at 8*d* or 10*d* a barrel until 1936, when they went on strike to gain the all-important extra 2*d* a barrel. Their cry was 'We want a Shilling a barrel!' The strike lasted two days and the girls won their demands.

It was not uncommon for the girls working at such a rate to incur some nasty cuts which were aggravated by the salty water, hence the Norfolk Branch of the British Red Cross Society established a permanent dressing station and rest room near the quayside. Casualties were regularly picked up on a circular run to the curing yards and brought to the dressing station for treatment, on a Sutherland's lorry with removable revetted seating, as pictured here in about 1922.

Fish salting and packing on one of the plots and curing yards which extended far beyond the Nelson Monument on the Denes, *c.* 1923. In preparation for the season thousands of barrels were stacked here and salt was brought in by steamer or made locally. The filled barrels were lidded by the cooper and stacked for about ten days, after which time the bung was removed and the brine poured out. The barrels were topped up with more cured fish then packed off for export to Germany and Russia. Once in Russia the fish would be sold and the brine sold off as a popular savoury drink.

One of the last of its kind ever to be made, this 30 ft carvel fishing smack is being built by Worfolk Bros at their boatyard at The Friars on the banks of the Great Ouse at King's Lynn, February 1957.

To help seamen navigate the difficult and often dangerous waters along the Norfolk coastline there have been guide beacons along the coast since very early times. These were eventually replaced by Trinity House lighthouses such as this one at Winterton, pictured in 1909. This particular light situated on the high ground stood a further 70 ft high, illuminated by a prismatic reflector.

Since the first Volunteer Lifeboat Stations were established in Norfolk during the 1850s men of the county have led the country with unique distinction and gallantry. This is still a rare occasion: the eight crew members of Sheringham Lifeboat *Forester Centenary* with their Royal National Lifeboat Institute vellum certificates. They were presented on Tuesday 6 August 1957 on the slipway by Sir Edmund Bacon, Lord Lieutenant of Norfolk (centre). Earlier that year their Coxswain 'Downtide' West and Mechanic Teddy Craske had been presented with Silver and Bronze RNLI medals, and all members of the crew had been recognised for their gallantry on one launch in extreme conditions when they rescued eighteen members of the SS *Wimbledon*, a coal ship that sank off Blakeney on 31 October 1956.

INDUSTRY

Pouring the molten iron into casts at Elijah Young's iron and brass founders, Waveney Iron Works, Victoria Road, Diss, c. 1952.

Gissing post windmill, c. 1910. The mill is shown on Faden's map of 1797 but it probably existed long before then. Gissing Mill was kept in the 1830s by John Brooke who used his own flour as he was also the village baker. In the late nineteenth century it came into the possession of Henry Whittaker Harris who installed oil-fired milling equipment; he also acted as assistant overseer and clerk to the parish council for many years. After his death the mill fell into disrepair and now there is little to show that the village ever had a mill.

Carbrooke tower windmill, c. 1912. Owned by Herbert Jeremiah Minns since he purchased it as sitting tenant in 1900, it passed to his son, Herbert William Minns, on his death in 1921. In many cases, several generations of the same family ran a mill until they were replaced by modern technology. Carbrooke windmill's sails were removed in 1932 but machine grist grinding continued there until 1942.

Arthur Edward Smithdale (inventor of the Smithdale Patent gas maker) at the bottom of the sail with some of his workmen testing the sails they had refitted on Horsey Mill in 1937. The business was founded in the 1850s by Thomas Smithdale in Norwich and later Panxworth. They consolidated their Norfolk works with the development of a works in Acle in the 1890s. By this time they were renowned as engineers, millwrights, pump makers, iron and brass founders and implement makers. They also proudly announced they were the manufacturers of celebrated Norwich mustard machinery. Their Acle Iron Works were a familiar feature of the town until closure in the 1970s. The assets and remaining machinery were sold by auction on Wednesday 17 April 1974.

Ladies of the filling and packaging department, with their works manager Mr Fred Collins (centre), of J. & J. Colman Ltd, mustard, starch, blue and flour manufacturers of Southtown Road, Great Yarmouth, *c.* 1922. Generally associated with their prize-winning English mustard production in Norwich, Colman's can trace their roots in Norfolk back to 1805 when Jeremiah Colman took over an old mill at Stoke Holy Cross to manufacture mustard. His great nephew Jeremiah James Colman transferred the business to Carrow works in 1856; at the turn of the century they employed over three thousand Norwich citizens in mustard, starch and cornflour production, opening other factories in the county to meet increasing demands.

Filling, corking and labelling lemon squash (note the lemons in the foreground) at A.J. Caley & Son Ltd, mineral water, cider and cordial manufacturers, Chapel Field Works, *c.* 1921. Despite also producing very fine Christmas crackers and stockings, Caley's name became synonymous with chocolate and cocoa production at their Fleur De Lys works in the city. After being conspicuously absent for many years the Caley name has returned to the city recently, with a new company made up of many of the redundant Nestlé staff producing excellent dark and milk chocolate again.

Upper floor workroom at Philip Haldenstein & Sons, shoe manufacturers of Queen Street, Norwich, 1925. Undoubtedly boot and shoe manufacturers employed the largest number of the people of Norwich from the turn of the century to the Second World War. At that time upwards of 12,000 people were employed by the shoe trade in about sixty independent firms within the bounds of the city alone.

Men at work in the turnshoe room at James Southall & Co. Ltd's new boot and shoe factory on Crome Road, Norwich, c. 1935. After the war this company adapted an old patent design, the 'Thomas Heel', and after a two-year nationwide survey of children's feet they developed a unique foot-measuring system and the famous Start-Rite range of children's footwear. The company is now known as Start-Rite Shoes Ltd; its head office remains on Crome Road, and they sell shoes all over the world.

The end of an era. These men are filling barrels at Bullard's Anchor Quay Brewery (founded in 1837) at St Miles' Bridge in 1960: brewing ceased there seven years later. Up to the early years of this century Norwich could genuinely boast 'a church for every weekend of the year and a pub for every day!' and it had several renowned breweries. People remember with affection the city breweries like Bullards, Morgan's on King Street, Young's, Crawshay & Young's on King Street, and Steward & Patteson's Pockthorpe Brewery off Barrack Street.

Making art easels, dished seat chairs and single locker desks under contract for London County Council in the mill at Barnards Ltd, Norwich, in 1953. Established in 1826 Barnard, Bishop & Barnard were originally situated at their Norfolk iron works on Coslany Street and were the inventors and original makers of galvanised wire netting and slow combustion stoves. Best known for their vast range of wrought-iron and cast-iron products, they were makers of iron gates and railings By Appointment to King George V and King George VI.

Boulton & Paul biplane advertising their sales department, c. 1920. William Staples Boulton was joined by Joseph John Paul in 1868 and with modern wire netting production machinery they built a flourishing business, diversifying into iron fencing, iron buildings and garden implements at their Rose Lane Works in Norwich. They are best known for their work in the First World War producing steel-framed buildings, and in 1915 at government request they produced military aircraft.

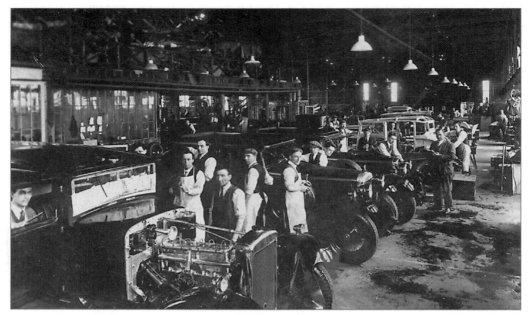

Motor car coachwork production line at Mann Egerton & Co. Ltd, Prince of Wales Road, Norwich, *c.* 1927. The company was founded by Gerald Noel Cornwallis Mann who purchased an electrical installation business in Norwich in 1899; he was joined in partnership in 1900 by Hubert Wingfield Egerton, a celebrated early motorist. They began trading in motor cars on Prince of Wales Road while the electrical engineering side developed on King Street. In those early days of motor cars their excellence in car coachwork was well known and they even built custom bodies for Rolls-Royce cars. Mann Egerton, although no longer on Prince of Wales Road, is still trading today.

Interior of the works of John Thomas Gibson & Sons, practical church plumbers and cast sheet lead manufacturers, on The Loke, Heigham Road, 1908.

Smiles all round from the girls at F.W. Harmer's new factory at Heigham, Norwich, decorated for Christmas 1947. A well-remembered clothing manufacturer, they made waterproofs, cardigan jackets and hosiery, as well as being Bradford and Scotch warehousemen, and making hats and caps at their St Andrew's steam clothing factory. Patriotic to the end, they made uniforms for servicemen in both world wars. Despite being bombed several times the factory soldiered on until it was burnt out by fire bombs in 1942. A new factory was opened in Heigham shortly after the end of the war.

The workroom of Johnson & Sons Ltd, hosiery and shirt manufacturers, Pier Plain, Gorleston, *c.* 1925. Founded by John William Johnson in Great Yarmouth during the nineteenth century as an outfitters, clothiers and boot manufacturers, the company diversified into producing 'every description of oilskin clothing for home and export' as well as a special hardwearing line of seamen's and mechanics' clothing and boots. They opened this factory in Gorleston after the First World War.

This wonderful study is the premises of George Smith's Stores, Norwich, *c.* 1910. He began just before the turn of the century as a corn and flour merchant and a pheasant-, poultry- and dog-food manufacturer on Little Orford Street. The shop grew and by this time Smith's Stores beside the Lamb Inn was one of the principal businesses in Orford Place, dealing in his 'world-renowned' poultry laying meal.

A fine array of agricultural machinery and workmen from Murton & Turner's Guiltcross ironworks, Kenninghall, *c.* 1908. In the early nineteenth century most agricultural areas across the county had the tools and few items of machinery they required made locally by local craftsmen such as blacksmiths and wheelwrights. By the middle of that century the increasing demand for advanced tools and machinery, spurred on by wide implementation of ideas from the agrarian and industrial revolution, small ironworks sprang up across Norfolk to produce the necessary implements and machinery required.

One of the most notable Norfolk foundries was Randell's St Nicholas Works, North Walsham; this is one of their many engineering workshops in the early 1950s. Established at Northrepps in the early nineteenth century, when the lease there ran out they moved to larger premises at St Nicholas Works. Under the guidance of Frank 'The Guv'nor' Randell (governor of the works 1888–1939), who foresaw the benefits of mechanised farming, all types of farm machinery and transport were made at the works until their closure in the 1980s.

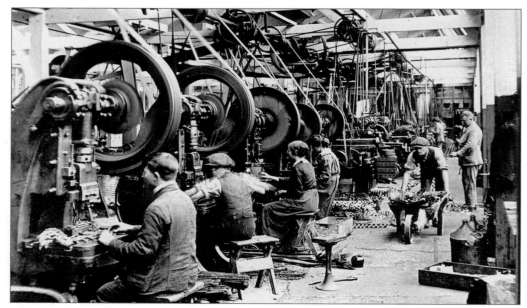

Power press operators at Hobbies of Dereham, June 1923. The huge shaft and belt system which operated the presses was run from a single gas engine. Mr J.H. Skinner started the firm in East Dereham in 1897 and it rapidly grew and occupied a large works manufacturing fretwork machines and kits, which were exported all over the world.

Castings of treadle-fret machines being made at Hobbies of East Dereham, June 1923. In the 1960s the firm was subject to a number of takeovers and went into liquidation in 1969. It was finally bought by Garrett's of Leiston but sadly closed down in September 1977. The name Hobbies lives on in Dereham as the sales manager, Mr A.I. Stroulger, set up his own business, Dereham Handicraft Co., to cater for the demand for fretwork kits. In 1980 Mr Stroulger was assigned Hobbies' trademark and patents and thus his company name changed to Hobbies Ltd.

The turning and shaping room of the Briton Brush Company, Wymondham, *c.* 1925. Briton Brush was formed in 1920 when S.D. Page & Sons amalgamated with Matthew's of Tottenham. The new company remained on Page's old site but extended the premises in the 1930s to meet the demand for the quality brushes they were supplying all over the world. In their heyday they employed over 600 staff. Brushes were made on the site until the factory closed in 1985.

Hats all round is the order of the day for the ladies pictured here working the Gane filling machines fixing the knots or tufts of bristles into the brush stocks and boards at S.D. Page's Brush Factory on Lady Lane, Wymondham, *c.* 1905.

Charles Simpson in his master craftsman's carving and tracery workshop at Cornish & Gaymer's Millfield Works. Norwich Road, North Walsham, *c.* 1930. He worked for the same company from the day he started his apprenticeship to the day he retired sixty-five years later. Cornish & Gaymer were probably the very best ecclesiastical carvers in Norfolk; their work in restoring religious buildings and great houses across the county and country was carried out in the very best traditions of the medieval carvers and can still be seen and appreciated today.

Craftsmen working the beams for the roof renovations of St Mary's Church, Worstead, *c.* 1900. Outside the church they created a temporary wood yard full of tree trunks. Sawn to shape the beams would be hauled up to the scaffolded temporary 'floor' just below the church roof. The whole roof was restored by hand by these craftsmen for the total sum of £1,100.

Woodbine break for workmen at Kidman's wood-turners at their Vimy Ridge works at Wymondham in the early 1920s. The wood-turning industry in Wymondham goes back hundreds of years and is specially celebrated for the manufacture of wooden spindles, spoons and other turnery ware, examples of which even appear on the town's coat-of-arms in the form of a spoon and spigot.

Sawing mill and yardmen from Jewson's timber and slate merchants, packing and case makers of Southtown, Great Yarmouth, *c.* 1925. This firm has today grown to national proportions as a builders' merchants, from small beginnings in Norwich in the nineteenth century.

Hethersett Cottage Laundry, *c.* 1908. Once a week it was wash day in the country: ladies would travel to the village pump or well, gossip and draw their water to boil in the copper at home. Woe betide the child that did not stir the copper enough and singed the contents! The laundry would then be taken to a common field where everyone dried the laundry in the breeze. Soon more enterprising locals realised there could be payment for this process and soon old stables were being converted to industrious laundries, with ladies smelling of Reckitt's Blue spinning the washing in cans with dollys.

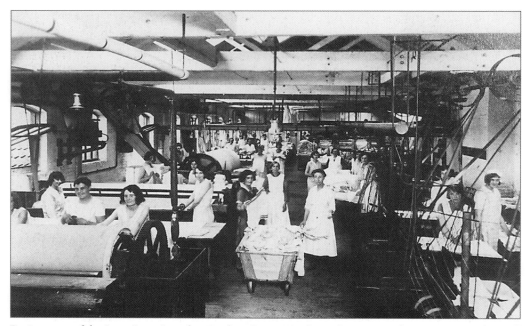

Drying room of the Swan Steam Laundry, Heigham Street, North Heigham, Norwich, *c.* 1925. Soon the small country laundries grew or were amalgamated into steam-driven purpose-built factories. The Swan Laundry was also unique as its steam engine also heated a public swimming baths attached to the premises. The fondly remembered Swan Baths were a popular Saturday morning entertainment for local children.

Stacking the cans for labelling and packing at Norfolk Canneries Ltd, Park Hall Works, 61 Hall Lane, North Walsham, February 1937. Norfolk Canneries was founded by Messrs Corbett and Duncan who began one of the first fruit and vegetable food canning businesses in the county on the site in 1931.

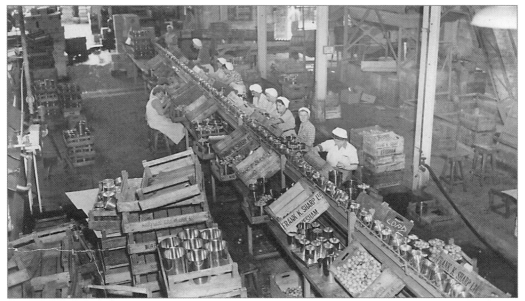

Canning potatoes at Norfolk Canneries' Millfield Works, c. 1950. By 1938 turnover had risen to £43,000 per annum which enabled them to purchase the site of their first factory and to expand further on to the Millfield site with larger capability and modern production line machinery. Hundreds more staff were employed to meet the demands of this expanding market. Although now sold to another company, the site still processes and produces millions of cans of food every year.

Linotype operators setting another edition of the *Norfolk Chronicle*, once published every Friday, *c.* 1948. After the lapse of the 1695 Licensing Acts, printing papers in the provinces became possible, and the combination of a wealth of skilled local printers and paper manufacturing mills in Norfolk meant that local newspapers boomed. When this photograph was taken there were still nineteen independent local newspapers being produced in the county, ranging from *Lynn News & Country Press* to *The Norwich Salesman*, alongside *Norwich Mercury* and the dear old *Eastern Daily Press* and *Eastern Evening News* which still thrive today.

CLERICAL & EDUCATIONAL

The Revd Arthur Temple Wardle (Superintendent) and the Revd Thomas Oliver with lay preachers and young men from the Wymondham Primitive Methodist Boys' Institute, based at the chapel on Town Green, c. 1910.

The Revd Vyner Noel Gilbert MA, of King's College, Cambridge, with the choristers of All Saints' Church, Horstead, *c.* 1907. Mr Gilbert was not only rector of the parish but also incumbent of the rectory, with a net income of £350 and 58 acres of glebe and residence in the gift of the Provost and Fellows of King's College, Cambridge, who were also by ancient covenant lords of the manor.

The Bishop of Norwich, Bertram Pollock DD, with clergy from parishes across Norfolk and beyond, in front of the Bishop's Palace after the service and act of commemoration of the 1,300th anniversary of the Diocese in August 1930.

Strong Victorian values and high moral beliefs can certainly be seen in the face of the Revd Joseph B. Alger, Wesleyan Chaplain, pictured at Thetford in 1917.

One of the circuit preachers and the orchestra made up from parishioners ready for Sunday morning service at Honing Primitive Methodist Chapel, c. 1912.

For many Norfolk towns and villages the first school in their area was the Church or Sunday School, so it was common for the first schoolmasters of the very early board or union schools to be clerics. It is quite fitting then that the Revd Robert Raven Young, the rector of St Edmund's Church, stands to the left of these Acle schoolchildren in 1894 with their schoolmaster, Mr Tallis Avis (who also acted as overseer), to the right.

Mrs Robinson, the school governess (standing to the right), with the children of Scottow School, lower division, in October 1913. Many of the children wear the uniform of the day: for boys it was a stiff Eton collar, Norfolk jacket, corduroy breeches which buckled at the knee, woollen stockings and hobnail boots which would spark flints as they walked to school. The girls wore a white pinafore over their dresses, lighter boots and just about every girl's hair was tied in pigtails or plaits with rag-ribbons, just right to be pulled by the boys or dipped in the ink-well for mischief!

Miss Clara Hobson (girls' mistress), at Harleston Public Elementary School for girls and infants, with students and visiting teacher instructors and their cheese and butter class, *c.* 1913. The Norfolk Technical Education committee set up and funded these popular courses, led by members of various agricultural bodies, from the turn of the century onwards. Other courses included dairying, 'Talks with Shepherds' and poultry-keeping.

Boys from Beetly & East Bilney Public Elementary School on Hungry Hill take part in a gardening class led by their schoolmaster John Hewitt, *c.* 1925. Even with agricultural skills included in country school syllabuses, 60 per cent of Norfolk people at the time were employed on the land and 'summer sickness' was a common occurrence. Parents would admit that their children were doing more important work on the land. This was a widespread occurrence until work on the land was mechanised.

The schools at Rockland St Peter, *c.* 1920. The schools were established in 1875 at a cost of about £400 for 120 children from Rockland St Peter, All Saints and St Andrew. After Forster's Education Act of 1870 which made the provision of elementary education a major responsibility of local government, elementary schools had to be set up where educational provision was lacking. They were run by school boards elected by rate-payers.

Writing chair and table made by ex-servicemen at Queen Alexandra's School, Sandringham, as a present for Queen Mary in 1925. After the First World War many ex-servicemen wanted to retrain to start a new life, and with government and benevolent backing a number of such establishments appeared across the county, instructing the men in woodworking and building construction skills.

A woodwork lesson in the workshop at Wymondham Emergency Teacher Training Establishment, *c.* 1948. Training teachers was one of the essential moves to get the country back on its feet after the Second World War. Many NCO instructors and officers leaving the forces moved into this field and emergency training centres were hastily established, like this one in Nissen huts on the site of a wartime American military hospital. In 1951 the Education Committee acquired the site and today it has become Wymondham College.

Begun in 1937 but halted for the duration of the war and only completed in 1949, this is the new Secondary Modern School at Cromer with the teachers, photographed on the day of its opening. Left to right: Mr D. Phillips, Miss P.C. Taylor, Mr S.R. Osborne, Miss P.J. Reynolds, Mr Barrington Boyce (headmaster), Miss J.M. Hudson, Mr W. Askew, Miss M. Parke, Mr W.A. Newland, Miss M.M. King. Under the provisions for more formal secondary education brought in by the 1944 Butler Act, existing schools were enlarged or new ones built.

This group is the North Walsham Secondary Modern School 1st XI football team in 1954. On the far right is George Barry Howard, 'GBH', the well-remembered sports master who taught several generations of local schoolchildren.

Housecraft room, North Walsham Secondary Modern School, *c.* 1957. In those days housecraft was the domain of female students while woodwork and metalwork were studied by boys. It wasn't until the late 1960s that the classes were integrated, often to the despair of the master and mistresses: boys were more interested in vim and flour fights than learning the intricacies of 'the wheel of nutrition'.

CONSTRUCTION
& PUBLIC WORKS

Sidney Johnson, stonemason and master builder, constructing the show house and office for Woolnough & Cogman Ltd at their depot in Poringland, c. 1955.

The old horse-driven pug mill mixing clay for making bricks at Cowling's brickyard at Barney in 1952.

Removing the fired bricks from the kiln at Cowling's brickyard at Barney, 1952. Once there were brick kilns near most of the towns in Norfolk, using the rich 'jambs' of clay common to much of the county. This clay produced the distinctive 'Norfolk Red' bricks familiar in the farm buildings and cottages across East Anglia. Cowling's was one of a handful of brickyards still working after the Second World War, but all had closed by the end of the 1960s.

The sawyer pushes down and the pitman pushes up (getting shavings all over him) in the saw-pit at H.W. Green's, timber merchants of Garden Street, Thorn Lane, Norwich, *c.* 1912.

This busy scene shows the sawmill yard of Edward Green & Son of Aylsham Road, North Walsham, *c.* 1900. Green's also acted as machinery contractors and their portable steam saws, as shown here, could be hired out to saw wood on works sites.

Workmen stand along the top gallery while some small children line up at ground level to create this charming study of the restoration works on the tower and eastern gable on the church of St Mary the Virgin at Winfarthing in 1912. The scaffolding is made from wooden poles lashed with ropes – note the height of the ladder to the right of the picture!

The last cathedral to be built in the county was the Roman Catholic Church of St John the Baptist in Norwich, constructed originally as a magnificent church and paid for by the generosity of the 15th Duke of Norfolk. It is seen here in 1908 in its twenty-sixth year of construction, with the tower scaffolding in place. It was finally completed in 1910. The church was given cathedral status by the Vatican in 1976 and its first bishop was enthroned the same year.

Constructing the Cantley sugar beet processing factory, 1912. Work commenced in March 1912 and the chimney was capped off by July; despite the site being awash after the great flood in August that year the factory, the first of its kind in the UK, was opened in November. The total cost of the factory was about £170,000.

The Norfolk and Norwich Hospital was founded in 1771 and largely rebuilt in 1882, since when it has been enlarged several times. Seen here in the late 1920s, this is the new eye, ear, nose and throat block being constructed from plans drawn up by Edward Boardman & Son, architects and surveyors to the hospital, of Queen Street, Norwich.

Bishop Bridge gas works and gas-holder in Norwich, *c.* 1905. Constructed by the British Gas Light Company in the early nineteenth century, this was one of the first major gas works in Norwich. It was quickly followed by the St Martin Palace Works in 1851, to meet growing demands as gas became a popular source of domestic power for stoves and lighting as well as for street lamps. In those days 1,000 cubic feet of gas would cost the grand sum of 1*s*.

Contractors pause for the camera during the construction of no. 4 holder at Bishop Bridge Gas Works, Norwich, *c.* 1912. Following the appointment of Thomas Glover (wearing the white coat and boater) as chief engineer and manager of the Norwich undertaking in 1901, he submitted progressive plans to convert the works at Bishop Bridge into a distribution plant, enabling gas manufacture to be concentrated at the Palace Works. Work got under way slowly and despite being halted during the First World War the works were completed by 1922 at a cost of £236,000.

This cable gang from Norwich Telephone Engineering are installing the wire to the magneto exchange installed in the sub-post office at Drayton, *c.* 1912. Telephones came to Norfolk in 1883 when the first telephone exchange was opened on Exchange Street in Norwich. The exchange was manned by a man and a boy and was open six days a week from 8.30 a.m. to 6.00 p.m., with a Sunday service from 10.00 a.m. to 1.00 p.m. following a year later.

The things we take for granted today were not available in the more rural areas of Norfolk until comparatively recent times. Here trenches are being dug for the installation of underground electricity cables in front of the Central Cash Stores at Martham in February 1931.

The City of Norwich Water Works Company's pumping station at Heigham, Norwich, *c*. 1905. Opened at the end of the last century, the station housed Sultzer, Patteson and Bacon steam-driven beam engines which pumped millions of gallons of water and powered the treatment works. The engines remained in use until 1929 when they were replaced by 964 hp electrically driven pumps; this was one of the improvements instigated after the Norwich Corporation bought the works in 1921.

Cutting the first sod for the new Wells sewerage system, March 1949. The two greatest problems for the county's public health provision at the turn of the century were the poor quality of drinking water and the inadequate sewerage system. Little was done until 1944 when the Minister of Health saw Norfolk as top priority in the Rural Water Supplies Act. By 1951 37 per cent of Norfolk homes were still without piped water and 40 per cent of households did not have exclusive rights to a lavatory. This is why so many local people can still remember 'the Honey Cart' which always seemed to call at Sunday tea-time!

MARKET DAY & SHOPPING

Crowds throng Ingham cattle fair on Trinity Monday, 23 May 1910. For people in very rural communities who would normally have to travel to the nearest town's weekly market, a livestock fair would be held within their parish's bounds once or twice a year on a particular day which seemed to have been laid down since time immemorial. Fair days were often connected with a Christian or even a pagan religious festival. Very few such fairs still exist today, the only evidence for them surviving in field names such as the Fairland.

Drovers and buyers survey the full sheep pens at Norwich cattle market, *c.* 1905. The origins of the cattle market can be traced back to the twelfth century while a second charter of 1462 gave Norwich a monopoly of market rights for 'Five leages of the saide citie and sircuit thereof'. By the twentieth century the 8½ acre site hosted six firms of auctioneers and thirty-three private dealers selling 212,000 head of stock and 100,000 head of fowl and turkey per annum. The stock market moved to Hall Road in 1960 and the original site was used for a few years as a car park, but is now part of the Castle Mall shopping complex.

Business is brisk in the Norwich Corn Hall, 1961. All trading was carried out here for over a hundred years under the portraits of Thomas William Coke, the farming improver and Norfolk MP, and John Culley Esq., the founder of the Corn Hall. The original corn exchange, built in 1826, was replaced with a new building, 126 ft long and 81 ft wide, in 1861 at a cost of £6,000.

Norwich Good Friday Horse Fair on Bell Avenue, 1893. The horse sales were operated here for almost a hundred years by Spelmans auctioneers who held their first sale in the castle ditches in June 1825.

Most towns across the county also had their own provision and cattle markets. This is Fakenham cattle market in about 1904. The market was built near Bridge Street in 1857. Market day for corn and cattle was Thursday, the stock coming under the hammer of John Long & Son, later Long & Beck, who auctioneered in the town for generations.

Timo Smith, the drover of Reepham, *c*. 1910. Since earliest times cattle were driven by track and lane to market; in fact it was not unknown for livestock to be driven down to London from Norfolk on the hoof until comparatively recent times. This was not popular with the farmers though as the animals lost so much weight on the journey. Drovers were employed by farmers to drive the livestock all the way to market, collecting on the way 'penny boys', who used sticks to 'tarn 'em back' from side streets and gateways.

One of the more unusual sights — and doubtless more onerous tasks for the drover and his boys — was the driving of fowl along the roads to market. Here a flock of Norfolk black turkeys are being driven to Attleborough station in about 1930.

A real agricultural, ploughshare and provision market at Downham Market, *c.* 1912. This market was held every Friday around the Gothic clock tower presented to the town in 1878 by James Scott Esq., grocer, draper and warehouseman.

As time passed the range of goods for sale at the weekly market changed from agricultural machinery and wares to provisions, haberdashery, clothing and domestic items. As ever, though, the weekly market provides the opportunity for local men to have a mardle and the ladies a gossip, as in this wonderfully evocative photo of Watton Wednesday market in about 1930.

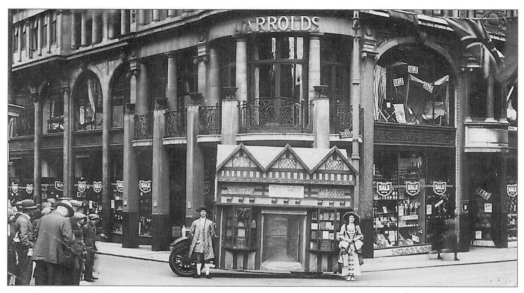

Jarrold & Son's flagship department stores, Norwich, c. 1937. Designed by Skipper and built between 1903 and 1905 on Exchange Street, the finishing touch is the display car converted into a mobile model of their first shop in Wymondham as it looked in the 1770s. For generations now Jarrolds have been printers, binders, fancy stationers, die sinkers and engravers. Now they have additional department stores in Cromer, Great Yarmouth and Lowestoft, but their high reputation for good quality and service has survived. Still in family hands, the stores flourish today as true Norfolk institutions.

Staff at the North Walsham branch of the International Stores, c. 1909. International was the first store to adopt a universal standard shop front. Such shops spread through just about every county town from the turn of the century and became familiar all over the country. Sadly, they seemed to disappear virtually overnight in the 1970s and 1980s.

The Norwich Co-Op Society Ltd was established in the city during the latter half of the nineteenth century. Pictured here are the staff of the grocery and provision side of the store (the other half was a drapers and outfitters) at 58 St Stephen's Street in about 1910.

Colkirk branch of the Fakenham Co-operative Society Ltd, *c.* 1914. Even in the more rural areas (Colkirk parish was home to 409 souls at the time) some of the co-operative stores were successful, with their reasonable prices and 'divvy' schemes.

The Travel Bureau, 92 Prince of Wales Road, Norwich, *c.* 1912. Necessary for businessmen and travellers alike, this bureau offered transport on the classic White Star Line (notorious for the loss of its flagship, the SS *Titanic*), the Royal Line and the Canadian Pacific Railway Company to explore the new world. From here you could send a parcel 'anywhere in the world', but a London–Paris trip took 6 hours 50 minutes.

Percy Kerrison (far right) with a few of the antique and curious bicycles outside his bicycle shop in Chapel Street, Norwich, *c.* 1949. The business was founded by his father George, known popularly as 'Dodger' Kerrison. After years of dealing in firewood and kindling from the garden of his terraced house and doing jobs for people in exchange for goods they no longer wanted, Dodger had saved up enough money to start a bicycle shop. The business prospered and countless Norwich citizens will remember with affection buying or hiring bicycles from Dodger's.

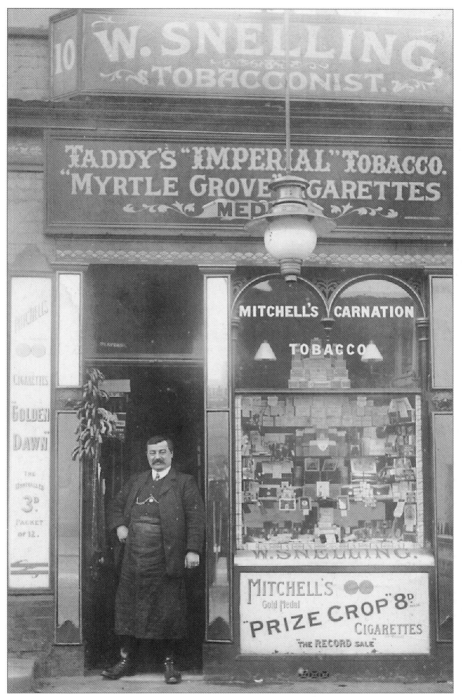

William Snelling, wearing his fine watch and chain, stands proudly in the doorway of his tobacconist's shop at 10 Prince of Wales Road, Norwich, *c.* 1905. Check out some of the prices: 3*d* for 12 Mitchell's 'Golden Dawn' or 'Prize Crop' at 8*d*; with names like Taddy's Imperial and Myrtle Grove, well before we knew smoking was harmful, who could resist?

These must be some of the largest cuts of meat I have ever seen on display, pictured outside Arthur Robert Wilson's family butchers at Burnham Market, Christmas 1910. I wonder what today's health inspectors would say about such a display!

Fergus Annison's fishmonger's shop at 2 Angel Road, New Catton, *c.* 1928. There is a very fine and unusual display in his open shop front and signs advertise freshly delivered mussels, cockles and whelks, and rabbits a speciality.

This fine study shows the shop delivery carts together with the baking, delivery and serving staff of Nicholas Bros, pastry cooks, bakers and confectioners, of 12 St Augustine's Street on the corner of Sussex Street, Norwich, in about 1908.

Jacob Howard, the baker of 12 Millers Lane, New Catton, pictured in front of the ovens his family had been using since 1847. Notice the fresh bread beside him and the tins stacked up at the window. This picture was taken immediately before the modernisation of the bakery in the 1930s into a 'modern hygienic bakery'. Always one for improvements, Mr Howard is believed to have been the first baker in Norwich to have a motorised delivery van for his rounds.

Cubitt's Stores, 21–22 Market Place, North Walsham, *c.* 1904. Founded in the 1850s by Charles Cubitt as a grocer and draper, the business rapidly expanded into wholesale and retail linen and woollen drapers, tea dealer and funeral furnisher. In 1887 his premises were extended and renamed Jubilee House in honour of Queen Victoria's Jubilee that year.

In the 1870s Charles Cubitt's son joined the business and this additional store was opened on King's Arms Street. It is pictured here in about 1930 with all the white-aproned staff posing outside for the camera. The store specialised in cooked meats, game and tinned foods.

Edmund Roland Smith, corner newsagent, tobacconist, printer and bookbinder, Norwich, *c.* 1916.
Always popular, such little shops were typically visited for the daily paper and a packet of Woodbines. The
newsboards reflect dramatic times at home and abroad from the coal strike to women's war work, as well
as news from the Front and 'Life in the Trenches', with photographs of fallen heroes. At the other end of
the scale, the *People* newspaper runs 'amazing allegations' about tea shop kisses!

Charles Harvey Standley's ironmonger's shop, 'The Little Dustpan' on Town Green, Wymondham,
c. 1895. Established in 1886, the shop dealt in glass, earthenware, china, lamps, mineral oil and paper
hangings, and offered a horse and cart delivery service within a 6 mile radius of the town. The business
expanded to include sales of bicycles, radios and televisions. Having passed down through several
generations of the family for over a hundred years, it was Wymondham's longest surviving family shop.

Some things hardly change. In rural villages life depended, and in many respects still does, on a few well-stocked shops, a sub-post office and a public house, as typified by this view of Cawston Street in about 1910. At this time the shops served a community of about a thousand residents.

Carriages and trotting carts in front of the Eastern Counties Co-operative Association Ltd receiving and collecting depot for eggs at Kenninghall, *c.* 1905.

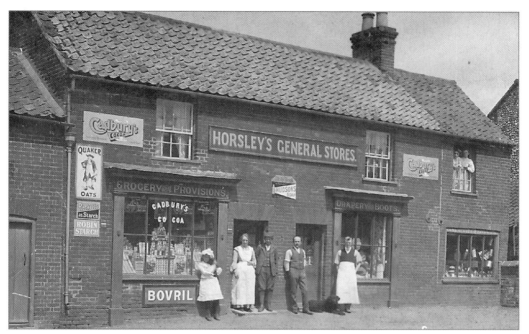

Horsley's general stores of Sculthorpe, *c.* 1907. Run by the local milling and farming family, the stores provided the village, then numbering 503 residents, with their day-to-day requisites of groceries, provisions, drapery, boots and hardware.

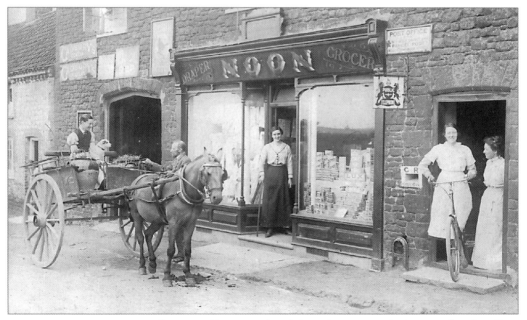

Mrs Annie Noon stands in the doorway of her grocer's and draper's shop, which also served as the village post office for Ringstead, *c.* 1920. At this time the population of this tiny community was 458. Situated 1½ miles from the nearest railway station and 3 miles from the nearest town, local people would often depend on their village shop for all their domestic needs.

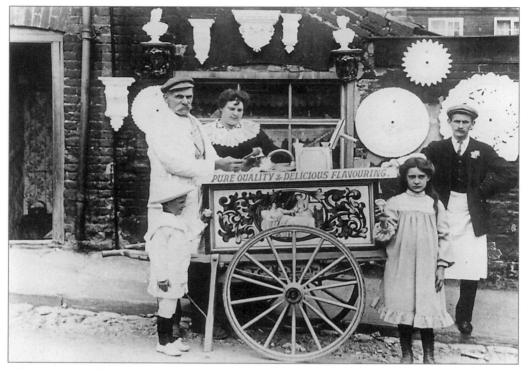

What better way to complete a trip to town than with an ice-cream? This is one of Norwich City's very first ice-cream sellers, Big Peter Chiesa, selling his ices on Ber Street in about 1910.

The King's Head Inn, licensee James William Wright, on the High Street in Acle, *c.* 1912. The biggest pubs in the county (outside the city) were to be found in the market towns. Often they had stood on the same sites for hundreds of years and many developed into coaching inns when the turnpikes came, but historically they were busiest on market day when the snugs would be filled with farmers, with drovers and traders in the public bars all mardling about the seasons and how they had fared, and exchanging local gossip.

EMERGENCY SERVICES

Some of the officers of the Norfolk Fire Brigade's Association photographed after their Annual Parade in 1937. Back row, left to right: Capt R. Richardson (Fakenham), Capt C.G. Wells (Sandringham), Second Officer R.J. Carr (Sennowe Park). Front row: Capt W.J. Beck (Sennowe Park), Capt J.J. Kemp (Association Secretary), Capt J.B. Craske (North Walsham), Capt T.L. Randall (Cromer).

A fine line-up of constables with the old sergeant in the doorway at Fakenham Police station on Gladstone Road, *c*. 1912. They were part of the Walsingham Division of the County Constabulary, one of fifteen Police divisions in Norfolk at the time, with headquarters in Norwich under Chief Constable Major Egbert Napier. In those days a constable earned £73.00 a year (little more than labourer's wages), sergeants £86 13*s* 9*d*, inspectors £110 and superintendents £170.

Patrol vehicles and ambulances of the Norwich City Police Highways Department at their Pottergate Depot, *c.* 1933. In keeping with most cities the Norwich Watch Committee commissioned ambulances and designated them a police function. Officers assigned to ambulance or fire brigade duties (all policemen had been trained as firemen since the 1890s) were paid a few shillings extra so such duties were quite popular. This ambulance service was carried out in Norwich until it was handed over to the National Health Committee in 1948.

The seven Talbot Ten two-seater open tourers supplied to the Norfolk County Constabulary in 1939. The cars were stationed across the county and used for general duties and mobile patrols. All drivers were given advanced driving tuition and were expected to set an example on the road.

Wymondham Volunteer Fire Brigade at their fire station on Market Street, *c.* 1905. For many years most towns across Norfolk had no form of fire-fighting appliance and relied solely on bucket chains between the nearest water supply and the fire. Although fires were rare, the lack of proper fire-fighting provision meant that some fires proved devastating to the towns or villages they hit. People learned the hard way from such fires and by the early Victorian period fire-fighting appliances had been well developed, and increasing philanthropic feelings at the time saw the creation of Norfolk's first volunteer fire brigades.

Firemen from Harleston Fire Brigade under Capt Prentice and Sub-Lt Perfitt working hard to control a fire at Lodge Farm House, Rushall, on Wednesday 12 May 1909. The fire was discovered at about 4 a.m. by the owner of the house, Mr W.S. Nobbs, who managed to evacuate his family safely and summon the police and fire brigade. Successfully saving the farm outbuildings, the firemen worked tirelessly until 4.00 p.m. that afternoon but all that was left of the house were the chimneys and main walls.

Reepham Volunteer Fire Brigade on parade under Chief Officer Sidney P. Eglington in the market-place, *c.* 1936. By this time all parishes in the county were covered by the services of a volunteer fire brigade; long before the days of electronic bleepers, when the alarm was raised the brigade members were summoned by the launching of maroons which rocketed into the sky and exploded with a massive boom that could be heard all over the town. This not only summoned the firemen, it also ensured a good turn out of curious locals to watch the engine go by.

Firemen of Sennowe Park Fire Brigade on full hose drill, March 1937. This practice was just one small part of the brigade's massive preparations for the International Fire Brigade Conference attended by twenty-eight nations and hosted at Sennowe Park at Whitsun.

The Sennowe Park Fire Brigade, winners of the championship at the International Fire Brigades' Camp, May 1937. Standing, left to right: W. Farrow, R. Pilch, W. Clithroe, W. Ebbage, L. Palmer. Seated: Second Officer R. Carr, Lady Cook, Sir Thomas Cook MP, Chief Officer W.J. Beck. Seated on the ground are Misses Geraldine and Rosemary Cook.

Firemen of the Cromer Fire Brigade demonstrate rescue technique using the ladder and cradle at the Norfolk Fire Brigades' Association Competition hosted by Cromer on the town football ground in June 1938. Anyone who wished to summon this brigade had to dash to the engine house on Canada Road and ring the bell outside the station.

Norfolk Fire Brigades' Association Competition at Hunstanton, April 1939. During the 1930s there was at least one hotly contested county fire brigade competition every year, with various disciplines including speed of changing into uniform and preparation for the call, drill and turnout, operation of the hoses, foam branches and ladder drills.

Officials and judges of the Norfolk Fire Brigade Association's competition at East Dereham, May 1939. Back row, left to right: Commander E. Cunningham-Glen DSO, OBE, RN, Capt L.A. Pett, Capt J.J. Kemp (Hon. Gen. Sec.), Supt W. Danzey, Mr Harold Bevir MA (Hon. Solicitor), Chief Officer W.G. Kemp, Chief Officer L. de Calvo. Front row: Mr H. Temple Owen (Vice-President), Sir Thomas Cooke MP (President), Mr H.W. Moulton (Chairman), Capt S.P. Eglington, Capt W.J. Beck (Hon. Treasurer), Capt T.L. Randall.

The Norwich Branch of the British Red Cross Society and the Order of St John of Jerusalem Joint Ambulance Committee ambulance and crew, *c.* 1920. At this time strict rules were employed across the county concerning which parishes could be serviced, bureaucracy dictating that a patient could not be moved directly across parishes but had to be transferred from one ambulance to another at district boundaries. This system remained in place until 1933 when the Minister of Health intervened, insisting on the free and unimpeded movement of casualties across the county.

Just a drill, and no doubt one of many, down the steps of Erpingham House, 22 Tombland, then headquarters of the British Red Cross, *c.* 1930. The sheet stretcher they are using enabled easier lifting and handling of a casualty (if he did not have a spinal injury) from room to room and down the twists and turns of an internal staircase to the ambulance.

Crowds fill the corner of the market square to watch the parade of Red Cross Nurses and St John members at the dedication service of the new motor ambulance for North Walsham Division of the St John Ambulance Brigade, on Sunday 23 July 1933 at 2.15 p.m. Funds for the ambulance were raised entirely from public subscription, since at that time, as now, the St John is an entirely voluntary organisation. The only paid members of St John were the full time ambulance drivers. For each call-out of the St John and Red Cross ambulance, the local authorities paid 1s 6d a mile, with a minimum of 10s a journey. From this money the voluntary aid organisations were expected to pay for new ambulances, as well as repairs, maintenance and running expenses and the wages of the driver. No wonder public generosity has been so essential to the survival of the Red Cross and St John – they were just about the only organisations, especially in rural areas, who could transport a casualty to hospital before the foundation of the local authority-adopted Norfolk Ambulance Service begun in the 1970s.

All the beds in strict line, all the corners neatly turned over and the wooden floor gleaming – a very formal and clinical air pervades ladies' ward 7 at the Norfolk and Norwich Hospital, *c.* 1908.

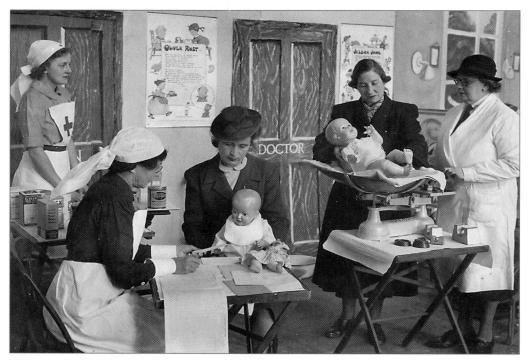

Red Cross maternity nurses demonstrate the facilities and services at a child welfare centre in a mock-up at one of the big Norfolk health displays held at St Andrews Hall in the late 1940s and early 1950s. Before the war the council had no such centres and the few that did exist were run by the voluntary aid societies, with the only real assistance coming from local government in 1948 with the National Health Service Act and the setting up of regional hospital boards.

WORKERS AT WAR

*This wartime emergency postwoman is pictured at
Edingthorpe post office, c. 1916. With many of the
young men gone to the war, work on the home front
still had to be done; thousands of women took the
men's places in hundreds of very diverse
occupations, from tram conductors to coal deliveries
and from railway workers to special constables.*

On the outbreak of war in 1914 many Norfolk men volunteered to do their bit 'for King and Country'. Various schemes enabled lads who joined up together to serve together, typically in the famous 'Pals' battalions in the north of England. On a slightly smaller scale, many Norfolk men joined en masse from one village or from an occupation. These men, pictured beside Britannia Barracks in September 1914, were shopkeepers, retailers and tradesmen who became 'The Businessman's Company' of the 8th (Service) Battalion, The Norfolk Regiment. They saw action in France and Flanders.

Munitions girls, dressed in their 'National Shell' overalls, from Caley's St James's Works, Norwich, c. 1916. The factory was turned over from making Christmas crackers to producing munitions. These girls had to be very careful to avoid excessive inhalation and contact with cordite, which turned exposed hair ginger and tinged the skin yellow, giving these girls the nickname the 'Norwich Canaries'.

A superb study of a young lady in Women's
Forestry Corps uniform, *c.* 1917. More than
50,000 women across Britain applied to join
the Forestry Corps and Forage Corps (later the
Land Army) between 1917 and 1919. Those
found suitable were employed in their hundreds
across the county, doing all manner of work on
the land from tending cattle to harvesting.

Lady Gurney addresses workers employed in essential war industries from the top of the tank beside the
Guildhall at the Workers' Day Rally during Norwich City's Tank Week, April 1918. Notice the placard at
the front of the march stating '300 women wanted for Norfolk Farm Work'.

Members of the Norwich City Corporation Engineers Department, 1939. In the late 1930s, as the winds of war blew stronger, Air Raid Precautions Committees were set up to ensure adequate provision for civil protection against enemy attack, specifically from the air. Air raid shelters and ditches were dug across the county and gas masks or respirators were issued for people involved in rescue, recovery or essential repair work.

First Aid Party members at the Thorpe Ambulance Depot, March 1941. Left to right: Bill Hewitt, Betty Clarke, Bill Howsham, 'Tiger' Harvey, George Cornwall, Jimmy Gant.

Loading pots and pans at one of the aluminium salvage collection points in the vacant shop next to Stephen Cooper's ladies hairdressers on St Giles Street, *c.* 1940. Norwich collected 2 ton 6 cwt of aluminium for the war effort.

A London & North Eastern Railway lorry collects paper for salvage at Fakenham, May 1940. In the early years of the war much was made of the people working together in a common cause. Salvage schemes were very popular, and cities, towns and rural communities were all encouraged to play their part, collecting anything from aluminium for planes and bones for cordite, or saving scraps for animal feed. However, a national team-building exercise was all it was for it transpired that the iron, aluminium and bone collections could not be used for war production and were scrapped or dumped.

The fire-watching patrol from Frank Price (Norwich) Ltd, drapers, outfitters and furnishers, of Magdalen Street and Botolph Street, April 1941. Most of the major stores and shops in the city wanted to be seen to be doing something for the war effort, not to mention being of mutual help by providing fire-watching patrols armed with hose reels, stirrup pumps and buckets, which might just be able to save their or other people's premises from burning down if they were hit by incendiary bombs.

After a hard day's work, many people continued to help the war effort as best they could, joining various wartime organisations such as the Home Guard, the Auxiliary Fire Service or Civil Defence. Pictured above are members of the Wymondham ARP quiz team in about 1941. Back row, left to right: E. Sporle, ? Whitehand, -?-, H. Tann, W. Clover. Front row: C. Woodcock, W. Corston, D. Guy.

The burnt-out shell of F. W. Harmer & Co.'s premises on St Andrew's Street, Norwich, 1943. The people of the city endured many air raids which killed people indiscriminately, blowing up or burning down properties. The worst raids came on the nights of 27/28 and 29/30 April during the 'Baedeker Blitz' of 1942. But these were not the last raids, and sometimes people had to face the disheartening process of turning up for work only to find a burnt-out shell. The people all pulled together bravely, making the best of it and restoring the situation to the best of their ability. Many of the businesses destroyed by the bombers were rebuilt after the war.

The Medical Officer and Red Cross Superintendent examiners closely observing the teams of doctors, nurses and First Aid Party members at the outdoor First Aid competition held at South Pickenham Hall Voluntary Aid Detachment Hospital, 1941.

Land Army girls leaving Norwich Cathedral after the Harvest Thanksgiving Service in 1944. The Women's Land Army was raised again in 1939, rapidly supplying about 85,000 women to work on the land. The work was often hard and involved all manner of tasks, but the women were renowned for their good spirits and thanks to them the 'Battle of the Harvest' was won.

WORKERS' PLAYTIME

Sing as we go! The workforce of Hobbies of Dereham leaving work in 1947.

Norwich butchers' football club, 1905/6 season. This is just one of the many teams derived from single business groups in the city. Butchers were one of the widest-spread trades across the city. With about a hundred shops within its bounds at the time, it really had pick of the players and thus went on to become a reckonable side known as Norwich Amateurs in 1910.

These fine sportsmen are members of Roys of Wroxham ('the World's Largest Village Store') Wednesday Football Club 1930–1 season. These leagues were so-named because their members worked on Saturdays and in North Norfolk half-day closing is mid-week, so shop workers could play on Wednesdays.

Steward & Patteson Ltd, Norwich Darts League Committee 1947. This photograph, taken on the Jarrold's Bowling Green, contains many local landlords – how many do you recognise? Back row, left to right: H.T. Browne, J.C. Fisk, W. Channell, H. Brock, W. Beck, A. Caston, E. Cousins, W.F. Browne. Front row: G.S. Moore (Vice-Chairman), J.H. Gunton (Chairman), D.C. Steward (President), H.A. Neve (Hon. Secretary), R.J. Paul (Asst Hon. Secretary).

All decked out with some of the popular adverts of the day – Fry's Malted Milk Cocoa, Reckitts Blue and Force Wheat Flakes (when it was 6d a pack), the staff of the local grocers portraying trade-mark characters are all having tea with Force's 'Sunny Jim' on the dray cart at Magdalen Carnival, 1925.

Works outing of staff from Reckitt & Colman's of Norwich, *c*. 1922. Such outings were always popular and in large companies each department would have its own. Fleets of charabancs would line up in front of the factory to take them to their destination, usually Great Yarmouth.

A few of the staff of the Briton Brush Company posing for the camera on the engine of a specially chartered train before setting off on the annual staff outing to Skegness from Wymondham station, *c*. 1935.

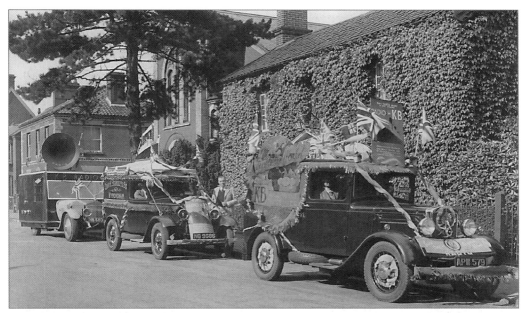

Eric Norton Standley stands proudly beside one of his delivery vans, opposite the shop that his father Charles Harvey Standley founded on Town Green, Wymondham, at the turn of the century. The vans, decked out to take part in the carnival procession through the town in about 1935, advertise Koster Brand KB radios who kindly sent their flagship display car: made to look like a huge radio, it was actually a converted Rolls-Royce!

Ladies of the Norfolk & Norwich Licensed Victuallers' Association Ladies Auxiliary on one of their many outings, this time to the Arthur Guinness Son & Co. Ltd Park Royal Brewery in September 1959.

The committee of the Federation Social Club, Oak Street, Norwich, 1958, with the 1958 Queen of Industry and her attendants. Back row, left to right: Alan Marshall, Jack Woods (Secretary and Manager), W.F. Vines (Chairman), Patricia Walpole (representing Norvic), Stan Palmer. Front row: Vic Wood, Norma Scarles (representing Norwich Co-Op), Mrs Vines, Elizabeth Mitchum (Queen of Industry, representing Macintosh Caley's), Fred Hammond.

Christmas decorations bring a festive air to Fakenham telephone exchange in December 1952. As time marches on and technology and business attitudes change, it seems that more and more people are required to work during public holidays which were traditionally strictly observed, although seasonal festivities were often encouraged to boost morale in the workplace.

The last presentation of twenty-five-year service certificates and medals to employees of the British Gas Light Company Ltd before nationalisation in 1949. The event was held at Suckling House in Norwich, and the presentations were made by company chairman Sir Henry Woodhall. The recipients were from town gas works all across the county.

One of the largest turn-outs I have ever seen for a retirement presentation: Steward & Patteson's staff from all departments pose for the camera on this special occasion in the yard of Pockthorpe Brewery, off Barrack Street, Norwich, c. 1938.

ACKNOWLEDGEMENTS

Good quality postcards and photographs showing Norfolk's social and working heritage are some of the rarest and most sought-after by collectors (probably because Norfolk people are too busy working to be too concerned with the likes of photographers); consequently my sincere thanks are extended to the following, without whose generous contributions I certainly could not have produced this book:

Philip Standley • Basil Gowen • Rhoda Bunn • Terry Davy • Harry Barnard • 'Gilly' Banthorpe • Francis Collinson at the Norfolk Rural Life Museum • Cliff Middleton • Eddy Riseborough • Chris Cock • Sandra Stutely • Anne Hoare • Elsie Kerrison • John Roper • Derek James and the Eastern Counties Newspapers Library Staff • Norwich Central Library Local Studies Department • Ken and Nick Allen • The M&GN Circle.

Special thanks are due to Terry Burchell for his photographic wonders, and to my families old and new for their on-going support and encouragement, especially to my darling Sarah for her love for this temperamental author.

Finally, but by no means least, thanks are due to the many people it has been my pleasure to meet and talk with in the course of researching this book. Every attempt has been made to obtain permission to reproduce the images in this book but owing to the age or anonymity of the photographers it has not always been possible. If any breach of copyright has occurred it is unintentional.

Three south Norfolk farm labourers and their dog take a break from their labours for their 'fourses' in the hedged bank of the field where they were working, c. 1935.